David

Probably on rising!

Catch a Rising Star

Best wishes

Robin

Catch a Rising Star

An Astrological Guide to Parenting in the 21st century

Artwork by Karen Nicholson
Cover and book design by Robin Heath
Edited by Robin Heath

Bluestone Press, St Dogmaels
Wales. SA43 3JF.

Produced in Wales
ISBN 0-9526151 6 9
First Edition, 2004

Catch a Rising Star

An Astrological Guide to Parenting in the 21st Century

by

Helena Francis

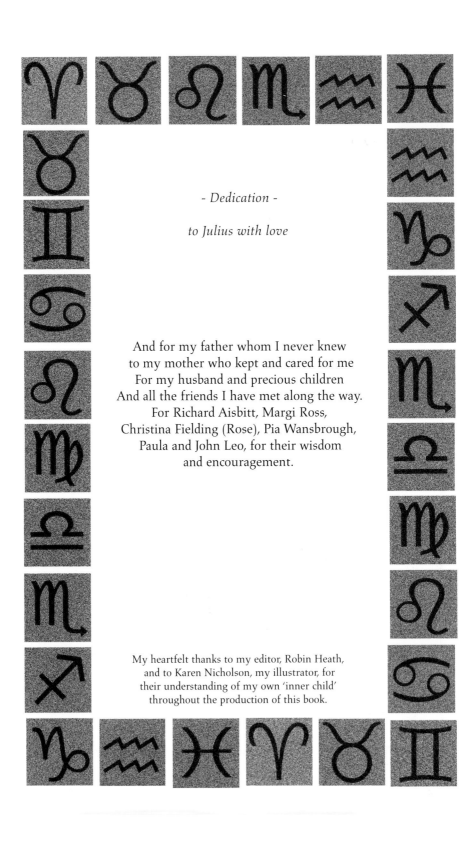

- Dedication -

to Julius with love

And for my father whom I never knew
to my mother who kept and cared for me
For my husband and precious children
And all the friends I have met along the way.
For Richard Aisbitt, Margi Ross,
Christina Fielding (Rose), Pia Wansbrough,
Paula and John Leo, for their wisdom
and encouragement.

My heartfelt thanks to my editor, Robin Heath,
and to Karen Nicholson, my illustrator, for
their understanding of my own 'inner child'
throughout the production of this book.

Contents

* The dates of the Sun's entry into each zodiacal sign vary slightly from year to year owing to the year being 365 days *plus a quarter day* in duration.

FOREWORD

by

Robin Heath

Former editor of the *Astrological Journal*,
consultant editor for *Correlation*, the research journal for astrology,

Do we ever grow up? Even in some of the most accomplished, gifted and seemingly sophisticated people there often lurks a small, misunderstood child that needs ... what? Well, social success is no guarantor of happiness, nor of 'being OK' in this world, and neither is money. Observing our society, as astrologers are particularly prone to do, it is evident that well-being and wholeness are not commonly met phenomena, and certainly not taught in our schools. A thoughtful person might well ask, why in heaven's name not?

There are many problems that beset our rapidly shifting culture. The technological revolution has increased our material comfort a thousand fold and with it our expectations. Meanwhile our emotional life is a complete mystery to most of us and remains back in the Stone Age. Twenty years ago, Helena Francis asked herself the question: *If modern sciences cannot provide an answer to our confusions, then can the ancient art of astrology help us find a solution?* This book amply demonstrates that it both can and does.

It is important that the reader understands that this is not the same kind of astrology that fills our newspapers and magazines. Helena has applied her researches to what has become known as psychological astrology. During the latter half of the twentieth century, the emerging discipline of psychology was allied to astrology, itself once the 'psychology' of the ancient world. Astrology underwent a massive reworking as many astrological ideas of the past were challenged and revised. The results were spectacular - the combination of astrology and psychology confirmed the validity of both subjects. Astrology used in this way became a more reliable decoder of human character.

We can serve no apprenticeship in parenthood, neither do we live in times where the well meaning advice of a grandparent will necessarily be relevant to modern circumstances. Helena's wonderful insights provide a timeless look at the qualities of being human, based on her practical experience of working with clients over many years. Free from obscuring astrological or psychological gobbledy-gook, with evident love, humour and without a hint of being judgmental, one can only wonder why her approach to understanding children this way has so seldom been attempted before. It has never been done better, nor with greater compassion.

INTRODUCTION

Parenting a child is one of the most precious gifts that life can bestow, yet parenthood is at the same time perhaps the most awesome responsibility that the world can confer upon us. There can be no more important priority than that we strive towards becoming better parents, and that we actively work towards a deeper understanding both of parental commitments and the needs of our children. Seasoned parents well understand all of this, yet the constant exposure in the media of the physical and psychological abuse of children suggests that many parents, teachers and carers fall short of that understanding.

There is an old and very wise saying which runs, "give me the child until he is seven and I will show you the man". Those first seven years of a child's life crystallise the future patterns of adulthood, the time when a new soul must learn how to read the environment into which they find themselves. It is these early years, before a child has understood the world and its challenges, when a wise parent must attempt to understand as closely as possible what are the latent potentials within the child. These latent skills and talents must evolve within the child's own manner of expression. The word education stems from the Latin *educare* which means 'to lead out', and this is generally misunderstood by even our principal educators. Astrology teaches and demonstrates that each of us is very different, and a wise parent nurtures that uniqueness in their child, right from birth.

Catch a Rising Star

Over the last half century, we have borne witness to the gradual breakdown of traditional family life. This long-standing social structure, the so-called 'nuclear family', about which it would take another book to fully discuss, did at least usually provide a reasonably safe haven in which to bring up children. Today, we are witnessing more and more children abandoned, left to the mercy of the State or to institutions. There are increasingly more children being reared by one parent or within relationships where several people may be asked to provide temporary fathering or mothering roles. Even the traditional male/female roles are becoming less well defined so that some children may be brought up by parents within same-sex relationships. All of these changes demand an increased flexibility in understanding the nature of the parental and bonding process.

I have worked as an astrological guidance counsellor for the past twenty years and during this period I have witnessed directly the pain and confusions that many parents experience in trying to balance modern lifestyles with the effective and safe rearing of their offspring. This begs some fundamental questions. How best do we understand our children? What would be the best educational programme for them? How do we cater for their emotional development? This book is my contribution to providing some of the answers to these, and other important questions.

Many parents believe that parenthood will come naturally, then recognise how demanding it is to look after their tiny baby, whose arrival can and does trigger an enormous readjustment of roles within both parents, with much confusion as to what's best for their child.

In their very early development, babies do not love their parents or carers because they are intelligent, gifted or good looking. They need their parents because parents mean being fed, being held and touched, and consequently feeling safe and protected. This gradually builds up a sense of their own body within their relationships with others, eventually that sense will enable the child to function effectively with others within a collective social situation. These early foundations are therefore paramount for any child's start in life and particularly so if they are to develop into well-rounded, independent adults capable of coping with whatever their future life may bring to them.

I became an astrologer partly because I wanted to know and discover more about myself and my energy, particularly in my relationship to my children. The study of astrology has been immensely beneficial to me, my clients, family and friends, with its deeply connected insights into human behaviour and motivation. Here's a typical example. Knowing that my son, Oliver, was born a 'double Gemini' (his Sun-sign and Ascendant sign are both placed in Gemini, the Sign of the Twins), has helped me to understand, adjust and co-operate with his 'Gemini energy' during his formative years. As a focused earthy Capricorn, I could feel myself becoming very irritated when my son clearly articulated to me that, yes, he could, in fact, watch television and do his homework at the same time. Just understanding his duality - the fact that he has in-built the ability to do two things simultaneously - eased a potentially explosive situation within our relationship. It taught me that I must honour and respect our differing approaches to life.

In reading this book, I hope that you will gain insights which will help you to better understand your child and to be able to nourish the needs of an emerging adult. It is so easy for parents to force their values, beliefs and ideals onto their children, always, of course, 'with the best of intentions' yet often with the most tragic of results. Kahlil Gibran's beautiful poem *(overleaf)* gently aligns us to a bigger truth concerning the parental role. Perhaps this book may help you understand your own 'inner child', whereby you learn to love and value yourself more, a process which can only reflect, once again, in a more thorough understanding of your 'outer child' - your son or daughter.

I hope you enjoy the journey we make together within this book and I wish you joy in discovering the wonderful insights that the ancient art of astrology can bring to you and your most precious children.

Helena Francis, Thursley, 2004

SUN-SIGN BIRTH DATES

♈ **ARIES** (March 21st to April 20th)

♉ **TAURUS** (April 20th to May 21st)

♊ **GEMINI** (May 21st to June 20th)

♋ **CANCER** (June 21st to July 21st)

♌ **LEO** (July 22nd to August 21st)

♍ **VIRGO** (August 22nd to September 23rd)

♎ **LIBRA** (September 24th to October 21st)

♏ **SCORPIO** (October 22nd to Nov 20th)

♐ **SAGITTARIUS** (Nov 21st to December 21st)

♑ **CAPRICORN** (December 22nd to Jan 20th)

♒ **AQUARIUS** (Jan 21st to February 20th)

♓ **PISCES** (February 21st to March 20th)

Your children are not your children
They are the sons and daughters of life's longing for itself.
They come through you but not from you,
And though they are with you yet they belong not to you.

You may give them your love, but not your thoughts,
For they have their own thoughts.
You may house their bodies, but not their souls,
For their souls dwell in the house of tomorrow,
Which you cannot visit, not even in your dreams.

You may strive to be like them, but seek not to make them like you.
For life goes not backwards nor tarries with yesterday.

You are the bows from which your children as living arrows are sent forth.
The Archer sees the mark upon the path of the infinite, and he bends you
with his might that his arrows may go swift and far.
Let your bending in the Archer's hand be for gladness; For even as he loves
the arrow that flies, so he loves also the bow that is stable.

Kahlil Gibran, 'The Prophet'

HOW TO USE THIS BOOK

UNDERSTANDING THE SUN, MOON & ASCENDANT BLEND IN THE HOROSCOPE

He turns not back who is bound to a Star.

Leonardo da Vinci

Under the roof of the Globe Theatre in London may be seen wonderful paintings of all the Signs of the Zodiac. Shakespeare frequently referred to astrology in his plays.

Symbolically, the Birth Chart is like a theatre in the round with the planets and Signs representing the players on the stage. Each one has something to say to the others and each make their entrances and exits throughout our lives. Some take centre stage more frequently than others, playing a more important role, but all the 'actors' are important. The three most important astrological indicators of character are the Sun-sign, Moon-sign and the Ascending sign, and this book will enable you to identify all three for any birth from 1960 onwards.

Put very simply, the Sun indicates what we *want* in life, what we are trying to *become*, the Moon shows what we *need*, while the Ascendant *points the way* or shows *the path* we need to follow to balance the qualities or potential of the Sun and Moon. Mythologers and Astrologers alike refer to this process as "The Hero's Journey".

In addition, The Sun and Moon tell us much about the parental influence on a child, and how he or she perceives the male and female energies as expressed by the parents. They also relate to the balance of male/female qualities, so crucial to our health and well-being.

THE ZODIAC

The Zodiac is a band or girdle of stars that encircle the Earth. This band is divided up into the twelve Signs of the Zodiac, very approximately one for every month Because our planet rotates on its polar axis, this circle of stars appears to rotate one revolution clockwise every day. The illustration on the following page will make this much clearer.

The Zodiac's stars are fixed with respect to each other over huge periods of time, but the Sun, Moon and Planets all move each day with respect to these stars and to each other. This movement creates a different sky pattern for each moment in time, and each location will further change this pattern.

WHAT IS A BIRTH CHART?
Date, Time and Place

Quite simply, a birth chart is a two-dimensional map of the sky for a given date, time and place of birth. To draw up a chart, you must know these three crucial pieces of information.

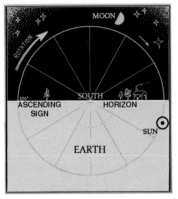

THE JOURNEY OF THE SUN & MOON AROUND THE ZODIAC

The Sun takes a year to pass through each Sign, thus spending about a month in each one. The faster moving Moon covers the same circuit in just under 28 days, spending just over two days in a Sign before moving on.

Each Sign rises on the Ascendant once a day. Because the whole Zodiac appears to rotate clockwise around the sky once a day, each of the twelve Signs appears on the eastern horizon - the Ascendant - for just two hours.

In the picture above, we can see that it is night time at the location depicted. This must mean that the Sun is *below* the horizon. The Moon is shown at its first quarter, and this places the Sun ninety degrees to the right of the moon, just below the horizon. It is *just after sunset*. If the Sun was placed in the Sign Cancer, (*midsummer time*) then the Ascending Sign could be estimated to be Capricorn, perhaps Aquarius. You could also estimate that the Moon is in the Sign of Libra.

> TO IDENTIFY YOUR CHILD'S SUN, MOON AND
> ASCENDING SIGN POSITIONS, YOU WILL NEED
> TO REFER TO THE TABLES ON PAGE 122 TO 125.

An example will assist here. My first grandchild was born on the 22nd December, 2002, in London at 6:12 am. The tables above and on pages 121 to 124 indicate that the Sun was placed in the Sign of Capricorn, the Moon was passing through the Sign of Cancer, and the the Ascendant was positioned in the Sign of Sagittarius. The interpretations for both Moon and Ascendant Sign follow on from the relevant Sun-sign delineations. Thus, if your child has her Moon in Taurus, you will find the interpretation in the section on Taurus.

When working with the charts of client's and friend's children, I always recommend that we look first at the chart position of the Moon. This helps carers and mothers 'tune-in' to their child's immediate needs during their early development. For example, a child with Moon in Cancer (a water element - *see page 129*) will have different needs to one with Moon in Aries (a fire element - *see page 4*).

THE MOON

- The Mother - Home - Early Development - Emotional Identity -

The Moon position on a child's chart can connect you to the needs of the child and how you may interact emotionally with each other. This position will indicate the automatic responses to the environment and the manner by which the child 'gets fed', on every level. Parental alignment to this will encourage feelings of safety and security crucial to early development, and will enable strong emotional roots to become established. Once established in this way, the child can then feel confident in taking his own life path, as shown by the Sun's position on the chart.

THE SUN

- The Father - Vocational Life - Personal Identity -

The Sun's position indicates how we might best give expression and form to our creative identity, how we may 'shine'. A parent who can understand the meaning of the Sun's position in their child's chart, and encourage and guide without overpowering, will be able to provide the kinds of experience necessary to enable the child to align to this developing sense of purpose in life. To encourage meaning in this way during the formative years is one of the greatest investments you can make into your child's future success.

THE ASCENDANT

- The Path - Perspective on Life - The Hero's Journey -

The Sign on the Ascendant shows the kind of path or journey we need to take in order to blend the qualities of the Sun and Moon. As a child is born, it is propelled from its mother's womb out into the world. From that moment a journey of discovery begins, and the child begins to perceive the type of environment into which it has arrived. The Ascending Sign is the lens through which we view the world, and indicates whether our approach to the world will be optimistic or cautious, direct or reticent.

As for every type of journey, the Ascendant path will bring challenges and experiences, in developing the qualities of that Ascending Sign.

TO LEARN HOW TO BLEND THE SUN, MOON & ASCENDING SIGNS, TURN TO THE EXAMPLES ON PAGE 125, 136 & 140.

TO DISCOVER MORE ABOUT THE SUN, MOON, ASCENDANT & PLANETS, TURN TO PAGE 126.

ARIES

The symbol for Aries is that of a Ram. Aries is the first Fire Sign and commences the zodiacal round, beginning around March 21st, at the Spring Equinox. The sign represents the beginning of a new cycle of growth.

KEYWORDS : *Competitive, incisive action, starters and pioneers.*

"Always look on the bright side of life".

Eric Idle - Sun in Aries

Aries

SUN IN ARIES

(Birthday between 21st March and 21st April)

Represented by the Ram's Head symbolising fertility and potency, Aries is the first sign of the Zodiac. When the Sun enters Aries, we celebrate the Spring Equinox (in the Northern Hemisphere), the time when the buds spring into life and new shoots sprout from the Earth, hibernating animals wake up and the sap is rising in the trees. We look forward with excitement to this new growth bursting forth from the rich brown earth.

A little Aries warrior is very much like these new spring shoots, which thrust themselves out of the ground, jostling and competing to survive and thrive. If they are to grow into sturdy strong trees and productive plants, they need to be nurtured by spring rains and warm sunshine. Similarly, Aries children need enthusiastic encouragement to forge ahead with their plans. Here is the key to the main parental role for this sign.

Being the *first* fire sign of the Zodiac, little Rams like to be leaders in everything they do. Competing (and wherever possible winning) is paramount. Always ready for a new challenge, being in front and victorious is very important to them. They actively invite challenges and often get themselves into very combative and competitive situations in order to test their metal.

Aries children usually display very self-expressive, competitive, energetic dispositions and very early on in their development you will notice that they are leaders and not followers. Their lively, extroverted personalities will equip them to lead or direct anything they choose to do in their lives. Never *ever* dampen or subdue your child's ardour and passion for life or you will have a very sad little warrior on your hands. Indeed, give them something physical and competitive to do.

Don't be too disappointed if they are not too interested in formal study. They will compensate with excellence in physical activities and sports. Aries children are bright, and many become highly qualified, but being confined inside a classroom to study might bore them to their boots, unless they are given challenges and, above all, stimulated into action.

Sun

Heroic stories that race along and appeal to their romantic imagination, with an exciting quest, are ultimately the kinds of experiences an Aries, young or old, seeks. Acting and drama are wonderful activities for Aries. Marlon Brando, who has both his Sun and Moon in Aries, typifies this sign with his powerful, non-verbal, physical acting roles. Ariens do however need praise, reward and love for their deeds, particularly for their courage and daring.

These children are basically 'doers', and unless they have the planet Mercury strongly placed in their horoscope, they'll be much happier kicking a football, competing in the gym or playing hockey or netball than being forced to study for long hours.

Try to allow your child to take a few risks now and then and try not to be too over-protective or appear too fearful, as this can be stifling to brave little Ariens who loves to test their daring to the limit, either emotionally, mentally or physically. If you can understand this single truth about their temperament and encourage their competitive spirit, they will have a very secure feeling that you are co-operating with their true nature. They are here on Earth to express to the full that go-getting side of their nature. Give them an arena where they can be in charge or be the director in any situation and you will have a very contented child on your hands indeed.

Your female Aries also needs something to challenge her physically - lots of lady Ariens have a natural gift for teaching physical fitness or aerobics. They need all the love and encouragement you can give them to develop these natural gifts, even if they express themselves in tomboy style and are often not girly-girly at all. Remember Doris Day, the famous female Arien, who starred in the film *Calamity Jane*?

Aries' planetary ruler is the hot, red, fiery planet Mars, which energises the spirit of the pioneer, risk-taker and adventurer, and they definitely need an arena where they can express and test their strength of endurance to the utmost, whether it be emotionally, intellectually or practically. There is a childlike innocence in Aries, as with all the fire signs. Their simple, direct approach to life is disarming and you will find that your little Aries will have the ability to help their more introverted or emotionally complex playmates to open up and enjoy the experience of really being alive.

Sometimes their direct and simple approach to life seems selfish and self-centred to more sensitive souls. Compromise is often difficult for this fiery sign but if you can encourage your Aries child to cultivate the qualities of diplomacy and charm, trying to understand and co-operate harmoniously with the other person's point of view, then you will have a child who could develop into an excellent negotiator, director, pioneer or leader.

Because most Ariens like to lead an action packed life full of fun and adventure, they need to learn wisdom in the use of their energy, which takes them time, and a parent, patience! It is important that they get enough rest and relaxation, so plan a quiet time during the day, perhaps reading them one of their favourite stories.

Robin Hood must have been an Aries and this story would perhaps appeal to their dreams of being a champion or a knight in shining armour. The pioneering spirits of Emily Pankhurst, Marie Stopes, Barbara Castle and Eleanor Roosevelt would be the Aries female equivalents. Every Aries carries in their heart the conviction that nobility is not a birthright - it is defined by one's actions and, like the innocence of the holy fool, teaches us that we should always treasure and nurture that childlike wonderment and faith in life which is truly the Arien's birthright.

Moon

MOON IN ARIES

Seize the moment, now will never come again.

Anon

An Arien Moon craves the limelight and being the centre of attention. Aries is the first sign of the Zodiac and being first and winning is very important to this charismatic sign. Linford Christie is an Aries and is a prime example of the spirit of the athlete who needs to win at all costs. Something in your little Arien 'dies' if they cannot win and be first, so great is their competitive spirit. Like Linford, always remember to give your child tasks that don't take too long to accomplish. Aries is the *sprinter* of the Zodiac and prefers to be the hare and not the tortoise.

Aries is normally not suited to tasks that require endurance and long term strategy. They like to see results immediately and patience is not one of their virtues. Aries craves to be in front and is a leader not a follower, either mentally, physically or emotionally, and is highly independent. "Thank you very much, I'll do it myself" is one of their cries. This is a self engendering sign - so try to encourage your Aries child to do just that.

This is not a reflective sign for the Moon, Aries Moon children are bound up with their own feelings and pre-occupied with themselves.

They sometimes miss what other people are saying to them which can seem a little insensitive to more delicate souls. But with a little patience, you will find your Aries Moon child has a vivid imagination and will bring their warm and direct personality into your life in a very positive way. Their emotions are immediate and an Aries Moon will express exactly how they feel in a very uncomplicated and assertive way. This may emerge as tactless, rude or red-hot angry, and tantrums are not uncommon with this Moon position. They can, however, be very perceptive to undercurrents of unexpressed anger or aggression in the emotional atmosphere around the house, so that their uncluttered and uncomplicated manner can do a lot to dispel those emotional muddles and undercurrents that arise within a family.

They will demand that their needs are met immediately - make them wait at your peril - this is an impatient "I want this and I want it now!" Moon. Like that great heroine, Joan of Arc, they always defend their emotional convictions and defend the underdogs in society. Just watch your Aries Moon child in the playground defending a mis-deed or an injustice. This is where you will see their true colours and their ability to deal with crisis in a wonderfully direct, honest way. Conversely, when things are running too smoothly, they will play devil's advocate just to see that the situation gets all fired up and brimming with action again. Aries positively revels in healthy conflict, just as long as they can win the battle and be the hero in their colourfully dramatic and romantic imagination.

Your Aries Moon child could be a little hot tempered when emotionally flustered and then act without due forethought. One of the best pieces of advice you can give an Aries personality, Sun or Moon, is "Think ten times, act once!".

An Aries child who learns to stop and consider their actions is a true warrior indeed. This behaviour can be difficult and painful to learn at times, but well worth parental encouragement. No one has ever said that Aries was a docile or an easy sign to tame!

Aries rules the head in the physical body and sometimes you can see the head of your child go down ready to charge, like the Ram, when passionate about something. Being a sign that is concerned primarily with self, they often take things very personally. Again, a little time spent explaining that there are other people who need to be approached with consideration and sensitivity will contribute to a smoother relationship with family and friends. Try to attend to their needs as quickly as possible - patience is definitely not a virtue with this direct sign. Always remember that your Aries child delights in the joyous expression of self love and self expression which can seem a little selfish

Ascendent

and self indulgent to the other members of the family. Teaching your Aries child about co-operation and sharing with others, particularly their brothers and sisters, is indeed a lesson well learned, enabling them to inspire others with hope and vitality which is the well-spring of life and reminds us more serious souls that to reject that quality of the adventurous child in oneself is to reject life itself.

ASCENDANT IN ARIES

You decide what you want, and you go out and get it.

Anon

With an Aries Ascendant, your Aries child should learn to project itself into the World with courage and self interest. With the hot, fiery planet Mars as their ruling planet it is important that they learn about sticking up for themselves early on in life and not being bullied. Learning to be the warrior and make a stand for themselves is the path to the 'self' for these children. Finding the adventurous child and taking a few risks throughout the life will enable them to develop this side of their personality. Life should be approached in an active, energetic, honest and straightforward way and your child should be encouraged to take decisive action wherever possible, particularly when their own survival is at stake. "Here I am and I need to be noticed!" is the message of this ascending Sign, along with "I have the right to be here!"

This Ascendant indicates a need for your child to be actively engaged in promoting the self - either by acting or performing in some sphere of life. Many TV presenters, film directors and other leaders have this sign strong in their horoscopes. There is a need to make an impact on their environment and a desire to present themselves as attractively as possible to the World - Steve McQueen being a good example of this aspect of an Aries Ascendant. Right from the start you will be aware of your child's need to be noticed so try to encourage them to take an interest in the way they approach the outside World. Some kind of physical and or competitive outlet should be encouraged, perhaps athletics, acting or a combative sport, such as any of the martial arts or motor racing.

Aries

Aries Ascendant needs an assertive, active and physical outlet to be expressed in a positive way. If other energy in the horoscope is compatible, then your child should have no trouble displaying and developing these characteristics, but if this type of expression is denied or repressed because other parts of the birth chart indicate a shy and reserved personality, then this could be a problem for your child and result in illness and depression. In particular, denied or squashed Aries energy leads to fevers, skin problems and migraine-type headaches. The key role for a parent is thus to find a positive outlet for this extremely forceful and physical Ascendant.

FAMOUS ARIENS

Sun in Aries

Jeffrey Archer, Kingsley Amis, Marlon Brando, Warren Beatty, Peter Brook, Charles Chaplin, Claudia Cardinale, Julie Christie, Robbie Coltrane, Doris Day, Aretha Franklin, Sir John Gielgud, David Frost, Vincent Van Gogh, Al Gore, Hugh Hefner, Billy Holiday, Eric Idle, Elton John, Niel Kinnock, Dudley Moore, Jayne Mansfield, Steve McQueen, Spike Milligan, Gregory Peck, Paul Robson, Diana Ross, Bessie Smith, Gloria Swanson, Rod Steiger, Stephen Sondheim, Omar Sharif, Peter Ustinov, Andrew Lloyd Webber, William Wordsworth.

Moon in Aries

Mark Bolan, Barbara Cartland, John Cleese, Dante, Placido Domingo, Sir John Gielgud, Galileo, Bill Gates, Whitney Houston, Jeremy Irons, Jacqueline Kennedy, Nietzsche, Martina Navratilova, Luciano Pavarotti, Raphael, Paula Yates.

Ascendant in Aries

Joan Baez, Barbara Cartland, Lena Horne, Janis Joplin, John Lennon, Bette Midler, Steve McQueen, Martini Navratilova, Nostradamas, Proust, Rasputin, Barbara Striesand.

TAURUS

The symbol is that of the Bull. Taurus is the first Earth Sign and is associated with productivity, stability, practicality and longer term goals. Taureans need security and to keep their feet on the ground.

KEYWORDS : *Physical, productive, practical, artistic.*

All poetry is putting the infinite within the finite.

Robert Browning - Sun in Taurus

Taurus

SUN IN TAURUS

(Birthdays between April 22nd to May 21st)

Blessed with a little Taurus child, born in the merry month of May (or the end of April), you might expect their personalities to match the countryside at this time of year, which is bursting forth with fresh lush green growth. But Taurus is much more to do with the long-term, steady rhythm of life and the powerful generative energy of the natural world. Taureans need to have their feet firmly planted on terra firma as this is a very traditional sign and little bulls appreciate the need for routine and careful planning. Why? Because this deceptively simple sign needs more than anything else a sense of tangible security.

The Pagan celebrations of Beltane (now Mayday) offer another clue to the Taurean personality, with the central maypole surrounded by dancers offering a symbol of fertilizing energy for the season. Earth energy is both strong and solid, and Taureans need to be productive and appreciated for their steadfastness. Their ruling planet, Venus, bestows on most Taureans, male or female, a great beauty which, although often rubenesque, is inherently glamorous and sensual.

Taureans love to absorb the physical pleasures of life, savouring them and revelling in their interaction between the environment and their bodily senses. It's a rare Taurean who does not enjoy their body! Physicality can still sometimes be considered unacceptable by the more traditional of parents, so please, please, recognise that this sign needs to explore the physical senses in order to remain healthy.

Food and massage appeal greatly to bulls, as too will music, dance, nature and fine clothing, in fact anything that connects them to the natural world. Taureans love sensual fabrics, so whatever sex, encourage your child to wear velvets, corduroys, silks and hand made designs, particularly those traditionally made. Taureans enjoy a developed tactile sense and also a good sense of colour, particularly pastel shades of pink and blue and fresh spring green which satisfy their natural eye for good design. The magic of touch and their appreciation of touch makes their hands very sensitive and many fine craftsmen and women have this sign strongly placed in their horoscope.

Sun

Needing stability and tangible evidence for their own skills, Taureans will often need to acquire objects. Wealth equates with success and validity to Taureans. Taurus children especially will often collect things, and *more* things, each imbued with a particular value to their owner. Because they will show at a very early age a liking for the finer things of life, encourage them to save their pocket money - perhaps giving them a money box. This will enable them to buy all those beautiful objects which give them so much pleasure. In excess such activities translate into greed and avarice, so a parent needs to show that sharing and letting go of things which have outlived their purpose is a wiser policy and will help to make way for more useful things.

Taurus has a reputation for being possessive, this is because they become very attached to people and objects. One of the first words a Taurus will utter is "Mine!" and you will find that once they get hold of anything, either practically or emotionally, they find it difficult to let go. Try to encourage them to share their toys and their time with other members of the Family as this will help them in understanding the value of sharing later on in their lives. Life for Taureans can become terribly clogged up if this lesson isn't learned.

Your little Taurean will usually choose the peaceful option in life, and are often slow learners and appear undermotivated. Exasperated teachers may tell you that they are not at all intellectual - even rather dull - which

is actually *their* shortsightedness! Taureans take time to get there, but no one remembers techniques better. This sign is able to take in the physical environment in a way which satisfies them enormously. In a pleasing place, they want little else than to just enjoy and 'be'. Their affectionate and peace-loving disposition leads them to explore that which is harmonious and graceful, and more than any other sign, young Taureans will often develop a keen interest in gardens, wildlife, art, music, singing and dance.

Taurus

They will love a walk in the countryside sharing the fields with the birds and the bees. In fact they will want to know the names of all the country animals and probably love a ride on a tractor - Taureans feel very much at home on the land. They will often know the names of all the trees, birds and butterflies long before other children and will revel in country life, enriching them with a keen appreciation of the earth and all it's bounty.

Take them out in the garden to smell the flowers and touch the texture of the leaves, particularly in the late spring when everything is bursting with life. This will probably be their favourite season. Show them how to plant and grow so that they can experience the cycles of nature and its seasons. Teach your young Taurus to grow the fresh produce they love to eat. This will enable them to get lots of exercise and fresh air which will instil a sense of security and further connect them to the eternal round of life.

Their placid exterior may be ruffled by several things. Bulls can see red when provoked too far. When this happens, and they do let the provoker go a long way before they charge, you will see their volcanic anger erupt. Then the bull will charge and woe betide anyone or anything that stands in the way. Then, miraculously, they calm down and forget all about the incident. Like a sudden summer storm, the lightning and the thunder gives way to sunshine and rainbows.

Taureans can also get disorientated if too much change is going on around them. Travel can be daunting and moving home can actually make them quite ill. A parent would be wise to let their little bull acclimatise to the new place before pulling the rug from under them in the old home. Taureans need firm and solid anchors under their feet. Taurus being a fixed Earth sign is rather like Stonehenge, that famous prehistoric monument in Wiltshire - immoveable.

Soothing a Taurus child, or adult is easy. They adore and need to be touched. Cuddle and stroke your child often, perhaps giving them a special massage now and then which will delight their senses. A big plate of food also works wonders, but you owe it to your child to provide wholesome and not junk food. All Taureans get the munchies and will eat what's available, so stock nutritious food, not chocolate bars and sugary things.

Now and then watch in disbelief as your little Taurus makes love to a cream cake. You will find that your bull will usually be very interested in what goes on in the kitchen and will want to know all about food and cooking. They may need to watch their waistline too. Taurean chef Anthony Worral Thompson, star of *Ready Steady Cook* is a fine example of this energy and many Taureans have a favourite restaurant or three, and love the routine of eating there. The composer Brahms always lunched at the same restaurant, taking the same table.

Another way to placate a bull is to find them a really comfortable armchair or sofa, soft lighting, good music and.. you guessed.. a BPOF (big plate of food). As a parent you just need to imagine an ideal seduction scene without the partner, (the partner having been replaced by the BPOF), then provide it! In time, as your young Taurean matures, partners will surely appear, attracted by their natural good looks, followed by their realistic and supportive approach to life.

Spontaneity is not one of their traits and like all the earth signs, Taureans like to know where they stand, so do let them know what you

have planned for the day, otherwise they can get very confused and disorientated. That is when their stubborn side can manifest. Change is often not handled particularly well and you really don't want to handle a raging bull, do you?

Taurus rules the throat in the physical body, and many of our finest singers have this sign strongly placed in their horoscopes, as do other famous musicians. Watch out for those dulcet tones emerging from the bathroom, or singing along with the radio and TV, and definitely encourage them to develop their voice in every capacity. Famous singers such as Cher, Barbara Striesand and Roy Orbison were all born under this Sign

You might find your Taurean child, male or female, trying out all your perfumes - they have a good nose for beautiful scents and aromas and will love to visit the shops to see all the pretty bottles lined up on the beauty shelf. Taking a keen interest in their bodies they could eventually be led into professions in the beauty business and fashion. You could also find that you have quite a vain little bull too, for the Goddess Venus was always before her mirror, so indulge them in a lovely mirror, for their appearance is very important to their well being. Audrey Hepburn who had Sun in  Taurus modelled for some of the finest fashion houses in the world and always paid a great deal of attention to her appearance, as does Joanna Lumley, star of *Absolutely Fabulous*, who has both Sun and Moon placed in this sign.

When it becomes the time for your bull to choose a career, this too may be slow in coming. Ponderous, with a great deal of inner inertia to going out into the world, it often helps to provide information, and experiences - guidance without too much inteference. Many Taureans develop skilled crafts, such as blacksmithing, milling, carpentry, tree-surgery and engineering. If you make sure that tools are available and watch for developing experience in their use, then you'll see practicality in action. Taurus loves to make, to build, and is usually very productive.

Fine wood, clever stitching, well finished items provide lasting pleasure to this sign. Many Taureans craft money, helping trust funds and stocks to grow magically, for themselves and others. You can seen many bulls succeeding in the money markets where the expression 'bullish' is used to indicate that the markets are profitable. The sign has a reputation for becoming wealthy, sometimes acquisitive, often overweight in middle years. As a parent, perhaps you might show your young bull the value of things without hoarding, how sharing gives

Moon

pleasure too, and how the simple pleasures are not always related to money or acquisition.

Give your Taurus child a secure base and lots of physical hugs and cuddles and watch as he or she grows naturally into a fine dependable adult. Taurus can usually be trusted to deal with the physical life and autonomy may come early for after all, that's what every parent surely wants for their child.

MOON IN TAURUS

"He who handles money well is an artist"

Alexandra Dumas - Moon in Taurus.

The Moon is said to be exalted in the sign of Taurus and here is a clue to understanding your Taurus Moon child. The Moon determines many of the main rhythms of the planet we inhabit. The phases of the Moon change the amount of light available at night, and are synchronised with the tides. These in turn affect the weather systems, and the Sun, Moon and Earth dance together like a beautiful and sustaining evolutionary machine. For a Taurus Moon child this symbolically translates into a need for total lasting security and harmony within the environment. Bearing this in mind, it would be wise as a parent to instil a sense of the permanence into the atmosphere of the home environment, ensuring that your child is nourished by the regular rhythms of life. Creating a peaceful and secure ambience is essential at this crucial first stage for this earthy Moon.

Even more than Taurean Sun children, this position of the Moon needs physicality. Moon equates with mother in astrological language and the contact between mother and child should be one of total safety, sensuality and warmth. Moon bulls are exceptionally fond of stroking and cuddling, but the experience needs to be framed within some sense of devotion and permanence. This is a very tactile position which needs to be nourished through all the physical senses. This Moon values things by their solidity, permanence and quality, and how these qualities are felt or sensed has real value to a Taurean, hence artists are frequently found with this sign strongly placed in their horoscopes.

This Moon position tends to imbue a good sense of rhythm, such that many musicians have their Moons in this sign. It is said that good memory is an attribute of a Taurean Moon. Fred Astaire remembered over a thousand dance routines whilst Hans Christian Anderson related all those fairy stories still loved by children everywhere.

One might expect a strong maternal streak, and your little Moon bull may surprise you with their ability to nurture and care for other children, animals and even yourself! In later life, they will make a very cosy nest in which to have their own children. Watching them play 'house' with teddies and the cat will confirm their abilities in this regard. Homely they are and if you ever move house, reassure your child that the process is not the 'end of the world', just the beginning of a new phase. Let them see, even feel their new environment before you decide to move or uproot them, or they may become ill with worry and anxiety at the prospect of upheaval and change. When travelling, make sure you take a good selection of familiar toys for your child who is unlikely to want to travel very far or very often.

Moon

Because they are so fixed in their emotions, Taurean children often have trouble with their energy levels, which oscillate up and down. It is important to ensure that your child gets enough sleep and regular meals. Food is vitally important in sustaining energy, and if you want to see your child wilt or become irritable really quickly, you will come to know that they need regular feeding.

If you decide you want to share some of that Taurean sense of peace and contentment then just provide plump armchairs, feathery mattresses, rich pile carpets and velvet curtains within an environment that is tranquil and serene. Your little Moon bull will blissfully share it with you and their other friends. This kind of contented inner richness links with the maternal side of the Great Mother and life in the security of that Eden-like state. For this child, the outside world is a challenge - and can feel very harsh with its bustle and noise. Your child needs to find the balance within the horns of this dilemma.

It is probable that your child will develop practical skills at an early age. These might be, like the Sun bulls, linked to crafts which promote productive use and stewardship of material resources. Karl Marx had both Sun and Moon in Taurus and wrote about the manner by which wealth was distributed and how money, resources and possessions were used and misused by people. Having good tools and facilities to use them could be a great gift to your child. Having access to musical instruments and free range in the kitchen may also nourish them in exciting ways .. but lock up the cakes and biscuits - remember the famous Taurean appetite and sweet tooth. Many Moon bulls, male or female, have an interest in clothing and fabrics, and become proficient at stitching, ropecraft or dressmaking at an early age.

No Moon position is better at teaching the rest of us how to be comfortable living on this precious planet. And if your Moon child is sometimes slow at learning, and dreads travelling or going to the city, they are perhaps showing you that there really is no place like home. In a society always on the move, you could learn a lot from your child and your life could become much simpler and more natural - therein lies the wisdom of this deceptively uncomplicated sign!

Taurus

ASCENDANT IN TAURUS

To be idle requires a strong sense of identity.

R.L. Stevenson

If your child has been born with this Ascendant rising, then life should be approached in a slow and steady manner, rather than rushing headlong into situations. Decisions can take their time! Life should be structured and planned enabling your child to systematically work towards their goals. Regular attention to the needs of the body should always be encouraged, particularly if the child has their Sun placed in a Fire sign (Aries, Leo or Sagittarius). This should entail getting plenty of rest and listening to what their body is telling them. A healthy regard for the body and its efficient functioning should be encouraged, with plenty of rest, good food and exercise. Most Taureans instinctively know that the body never lies and that it lets  you know immediately what it needs - if you can listen to what the body is saying. And this Ascendant knows how to listen!

Because Taurus is a fixed Earth sign, there could be a propensity to hold on too long to situations and things, so it is necessary with this Ascendant to learn when to hold on and when to let go, particularly when things need to change or have outlived their purpose in their lives. This Ascendant confers common sense and encourages realism in coping with and managing money and resources. Learning and incorporating the material lessons of life is essential with this

Ascendant

Ascendant as your child needs to experience the concrete and tangible results of their efforts in the world at an early age. Encourage this, and all will be well.

With the sign of the Bull rising, there could be signs of indolence and laziness, faults that stalk both Taurus Sun and Moon. A Taurean innately senses that being still is fine. But this stillness isn't really laziness while some Taureans do go too far with indecision and idleness, which should be discouraged as a bad habit and a waste of those wonderful gifts that are the birthright of this extremely resourceful sign. Activity can be balanced with peace and safety to ground the life, so that the more productive and artistic side of this Ascending Sign can shine through.

Art, music, fashion, design, interior decor or singing and dancing are often in evidence, as we experienced in the life of Taurean ballet dancer Margot Fontaine, and some fine engineers and crafts-people have Taurus rising. As a parent, the golden rule is to provide resources to prime the interests of your little Taurean, whether the sign contains Sun, Moon or Ascendant. Provide the good soil and then read the Parable of the Sower to understand what you have set in motion. You will probably relax in your old age as the productive fruits of your offspring are shared and enjoyed amongst their family and friends.

FAMOUS TAUREANS

Sun in Taurus

Fred Astaire, Buddha, Robert Browning, Bert Bacharach, Thomas Beecham, Michael Barrymore, Brahms, Balzac, James Barrie, Charlotte Bronte, Anne Boleyn, Catherine the Great, Oliver Cromwell, Judy Collins, Gary Cooper, Cher, Salvador Dali, Lonnie Donegan, Donovan, Sheena Easton, Ella Fitzgerald, Sigmund Freud, Henry Fonda, Albert Finney, Stewart Granger, Engelbert Humperdinck, Audrey Hepburn, Katherine Hepburn, David Icke, Glenda Jackson, Maureen Lipman, Joanna Lumley, Edward Lear, Liberace, Joe Louis, George Lucas, Eric Morecombe, Marconi, Shirley Maclaine, Golda Meir, Karl Marx, Yehudi Menuhin, Ryan O'Neal, Jack Nicholson, Roy Orbison, Chris Patten,

Taurus

Al Pacino, Michelle Pfieffer, Prokofiev, Dame Margaret Rutherford, Robespierre, Dr. Benjamin Spock, Barbara Streisand, James Stewart, Alan Titchmarsh, Tchaikovsky, Harry S. Trueman, Shirley Temple, Leonardo da Vinci, Rudolf Valentino, Stevie Wonder, Victoria Wood, Tammy Wynette, Duke of Wellington, Orson Wells, Paula Yates, Queen Elizabeth II.

Moon in Taurus

Alexandra Dumas, Bob Dylan, Buddha, Irving Berlin, Carrie Fisher, F.Scott Fitzgerald, Greta Garbo, Stewart Granger, Katherine Hepburn, Elton John, Joanna Lumley, Ian McShane, Karl Marx, Florence Nightingale, Prince Charles, George Peppard, Gregory Peck, Patricia Routledge, Diana Ross, Peter Sellers, George Bernard Shaw, Meryl Streep, Dionne Warwick.

Ascendant in Taurus

Fred Astaire, Hans Christian Anderson, Beethovan, Edgar Cayce, Edison, Mia Farrow, Carl Jung, Robert Kennedy, Vivian Leigh, George Lucas, Lisa Minelli, Percy Shelley, Dionne Warwick, Stevie Winwood.

GEMINI

The symbol is that of the Twins. Gemini is the first Air Sign and is associated with travel and communication, language and writing. Geminians need information and activity - to keep their minds busy.

KEYWORDS: *Multi-tasking, duplicitous, movers, networkers.*

The Bible tells us to love our neighbours, and also to love our enemies; probably because they are generally the same people.

G.K. Chesterton

Gemini

SUN IN GEMINI

There are always two sides to each question and really in life one needs a face for each side.

Anna Karenina - Tolstoy

Whoever wrote the lines 'He who bonds to himself a joy, doth the winged life destroy, he who catches joy as it flies, lives to eternity's sunrise', must have been a Gemini. This is the first Air sign, the glyph symbolising the Twins and representing the duality of the sign - 'never two minds alike'. The two columns represent the bridge between the human and the divine.

Like the chameleon, Geminians adapt to their environment, changing their colours to suit the social conditions. This sign is also the butterfly of the Zodiac and like this delicate creature that flutters from flower to flower, feeding and fertilising, a Gemini child will be interested in everything and everybody - which makes them very social little butterflies indeed! Here today and gone tomorrow - that is the nature of their presence and their calling card. Never try to restrict or fence in your delicate and finely tuned butterfly for they need a mentally active and ever changing environment in which to experience their lives.

If you think of the light changeable breezes of Summer you'll get the feel of your child's delicate and finely tuned nature. Gemini is the sign of the Twins and you'll often see your child talking to their other twin, either an actual twin (many twins are born under this sign) or to an imaginary friend, brother or sister. Try to encourage them to develop this duality in a constructive way. Gemini is a mutable sign, thriving on change, and is extremely sensitive to the duality of life with all its complex choices. They actually do appreciate that there are always two sides to a story and sometimes this makes it difficult for them to make up their minds when making important decisions.

Life is never black and white to a Gemini and this can be difficult for their often over-active minds. Furthermore, today's black may become tomorrow's white, such is the changing perspective of the Gemini mentality. Ruled by the mind planet Mercury, right from the very beginning of parenthood you will notice that you have a very inquisitive and talkative child on your hands. The other Mercury ruled sign, earthy Virgo, loves knowledge in order to then realistically apply it, whilst often Gemini just enjoys the sound of words and communication because it's fun and it gives them a chance to air their views - so necessary to their sense of self-expression. Words and communication are very important to Gemini and it is important that you provide a good education for your Gemini child, enabling them to develop their speaking and writing skills.

Geminians often pride themselves on their ability to use words to great effect and paying attention to this and to their writing skills is of

prime importance. They will delight in presenting you with a well written letter, story or account of what went on during the day. As a parent, such early attempts at effectively conveying information need to be vigorously encouraged. Parents need also to help these children discipline and focus their often over-active minds. Without this skill Geminians can become confused and may be distracted from finishing a task. This is why they are often known as 'jack of all trades, master of none'. Remember the butterfly and you'll understand! Help to channel your child's creative minds through communication skills with reading, writing, logic, even teaching, acting and counselling, all occupations associated with this potentially rational and versatile sign. Some of our most famous story tellers and writers are born under this sign, Thomas Hardy (*Far from the Madding Crowd*) and Ian Fleming (the James Bond books and films) to name but two.

Being a born communicator and having a way with words, always make sure that you provide the best education and stimulation you can in the formative years for your Gemini-child, making full use of their restless and inquisitive minds. Place plenty of encyclopaedic, puzzle and mentally stimulating books in your child's bedroom. Computers are a must too!

Gemini

Gemini is the sign associated with our immediate environment and what we have absorbed from early conditioning as children. This includes our relationship with our siblings and friends which can colour and influence our whole attitude to life. You will find that your little Gemini will be interested in what goes on in the neighbourhood and will want to come home from school and tell you all the news of what went on during the day, recounting their experiences with tremendous wit and humour. Gemini is a wonderful observer of local life and makes a wonderful mimic. You will find that they can copy almost every dialect in the land with their good ear for words and sound. Lawrence Olivier (Sun in Gemini) was a good example of this, displaying these qualities by being one of our finest actors and performers.

Gemini rules the hands and many make talented magicians and jugglers. In fact Geminians are very good at all kinds of ball games, perhaps not the heavy games like rugby, but more a winger in football, like George Best (Sun in Gemini). Tennis, basketball and badminton suit the personality, as Gemini really tunes in with the rhythm of the ball passing backwards and forwards between players. Steffi Graf, one of our  finest tennis stars has her Sun and Ascendant in this sign. Try not to restrict your restless and versatile child too much - they need a constant supply of fresh stimuli - and remember that they can indeed do two things at once.

The duality of this sign enables them to develop a 'second string to their bow', one of the most important things you need to understand about your clever, adaptable child. With their love of travel, words and language, it is important to encourage them to be as mobile as possible. Many Gemini children grow up to be fine writers, translators and broadcasters, particularly interested in the everyday script of soap operas, which focuses in on local life and so popular today. Gemini rules the media and lots are drawn to broadcasting, radio and TV. Many make fine teachers, particularly to the younger age groups, as they instinctively tune in to impressionable young minds. They can often provide information and mental stimulus better than any other sign.

Moon

With so much emphasis on mental stimuli, it is important for Gemini to get enough rest and relaxation, preferably away from all stimulus, where they can recharge their effervescent batteries, ready to meet the next interesting and interested person or situation. Often they cannot sit still, and fidget or talk continually when their nervous system goes into overdrive mode. However, you will find that your Mercury child is never dull and that their curiosity knows no bounds. If you leave the door open for them to explore their colourful world, they will always return to you with a humorous and witty account of their daily experiences.

MOON IN GEMINI

When I grow up I want to be a little boy/girl.

Anon.

As you look at your Gemini Moon child, you may be convinced that you are seeing double or that you have two for the price of one or that you have doubled your investment. Gemini is the Sign of the Twins and like their symbol, the two columns, representing the human and the divine, mortal and immortal, it literally means 'never two minds alike'. You will notice your Gemini child arguing and debating with themselves which makes it difficult for them to make up their minds about anything. This is because they *can* see two sides of the story and

this sometimes makes it hard to pin them down when a firm decision is necessary. Because of their duality, you will find that your Gemini child constantly fluctuates and changes its mind when confronted with a choice of some kind. Do try to understand that this is because they can always see the benefits of both

sides of the debate or discussion, a gift making them fine mediators in any situation.

This is a highly strung and finely tuned Moon and it is important to remember that here it resides in an air sign which connects lunar emotions to our mind and thought patterns. It can sometimes be difficult for this sign to access its emotions, for thinking is not the same as feeling. Geminians can often tell you what they think, but not how they feel, so it would be as well to encourage them from a very early age to try to express their feelings as demonstrably as possible, otherwise your child may feel a little isolated from time to time.

Clever and versatile, and with wonderful imaginations, you will find your Gemini Moon-child is a natural at telling stories or writing plays and is a wonderful mimic. And with this Moon position, as they grow they can become very butterfly-like, flitting from one social situation to another! You will also find that they remember all the little things that they've encountered during their day and have a wonderful recall for what people said and just how they said it. Moon Gemini children should be encouraged to develop this gift, perhaps directing it into writing children's stories or keeping a diary or journal of the days events - this Moon is a keen observer of people's gestures and habits.

They will love making you laugh and have a keen sense of humour. Many comedians (Bob Monkhouse and Bob Hope) were born with the Sun or the Moon in Gemini. Their tremendous wit and humour light up life and endear them to all their friends.

You will find that their brothers and sisters and their friends are very important to this Moon position. There usually is a tremendous bond with a brother, sister or special friend. There could be sibling

Moon

rivalry or problems with a brother or sister, but either way their relationship with them will be very important. As this is the sign of a dual personality, it would help you if you understood their need to develop a close bond with a friend who can mirror back to them their imaginary 'twin' to satisfy the need to balance both the male and female dynamic strongly associated with this dual sign. Because of this Moon's sensitive and highly strung temperament, it is important to encourage your child to understand the function of the mind and the nervous system, otherwise nerves can get a little frayed or run ragged, leading to nervous exhaustion and a complete need for rest. When your little butterfly is worn out, try to provide a peaceful environment for the nervous system to recharge and catch up.

Help your Gemini Moon to control their over-active minds and imaginations by channelling the energy constructively and usefully. As Gemini is associated with the lungs and the nervous system, try to encourage them to get plenty of exercise and fresh air and discourage them from smoking when they grow up, so that they can breath in that wonderful fresh air which they need so much.

Gemini

Gemini Moon is often a grazer or a snacker and may prefer to eat on the wing, so try to understand this and provide food that doesn't take too long to eat, yet is nutritious. Try to feed your child little and often, as they often eat like a bird and can be frequently distracted by all the things happening around them, so that they lose interest in the food. This can be frustrating for caring mums!

As your child gets older, you'll find that they are always on the phone and will be interested in all the new gadgets and new technology and techniques. "How does it work?" should be printed on a T-shirt for your child, to save repetition. You'll most probably need two phones - it is like a lifeline to them and enables them to speak to people lightly, often and sometimes superficially, especially to detract them from their sometimes difficult-to-access feelings. Gemini is not a sign of great depth and intensity, so don't expect your child to be absorbed by the more serious side of life. Gemini Moon loves to be free to play and explore their delightful imaginations which enable them to creatively reflect and respond to life around them. This child is never still and like the beautiful butterfly will be here today, and gone tomorrow, but you will feel better for the contact, which will often refresh and delight your day. Quicksilver (Mercury) is a liquid which reflects its immediate environment like a mirror, and many Geminians have this gift. Never try restricting their delicate and fine nature and you will have a very appreciative child who blesses you with all the jewelled colours of their multi-faceted rainbows!

ASCENDANT IN GEMINI

Listen, or your tongue will make you deaf.
Old North American Indian saying

With this sign on the Ascendant, life should be approached with curiosity and inquisitiveness. The assets of this sign are versatility and adaptability, but can give rise to the 'Jack of all trades, master of none' type of personality - which can be seemingly shallow. In fact, quite a party animal - Gemini hates to lose out on alternatives and being committed to just one thing or just one person means excluding so many other possibilities. Your child will display traits of duality and

Ascendant

there will be two distinct faces, only one of which will be presented to the World. As a parent, you may be lucky to see both, but the one hidden to the outside world will be yours to explore with your child. This can either be a curse or a blessing, but with the right support, this

duality can be effectively utilised in the fields of acting, story telling, broadcasting or working in the media. Taxi driving and travel agency could be suitable professions, facilitating mobility and an environment which changes often to suit this mutable Ascending sign.

Encourage your child to develop their mind and thought patterns in the fields of communication through speaking, writing, teaching and in the exchange of ideas, circulating information that will lead to positive growth rather than nervous confusion and negativity. Discourage idle chatter and gossip as your child matures. This will bring practical and focused benefits to themselves and others. Relationships with siblings and how they interact with their local environment and the people in that environment will be important to their development. Children with this Ascendant usually have the ability to eventually serve their local environment through their mental endeavours showing genuine interest in the welfare of their local environment, often concerning the younger members of Society.

Geminians can be active traders and marketeers, and Geminis are great networkers having a talent for bringing people, goods, services and ideas together. Like their symbol, the bridge, they are often excellent negotiators and mediators. All of these gifts should be encouraged and rewarded. With this mutable Ascendant they should and probably will telephone the world, email everyone and surf the internet! Watch the phone bill!

Gemini

FAMOUS GEMINIANS

Sun in Gemini

John Barrymore, Bjorn Borg, Zola Budd, George Bush, Cilla Black, Arnold Bennett, Joan Collins, Bob Dylan, Albrecht Durer, Miles Davis, Arthur Conan Doyle, Clint Eastwood, Ian Fleming, Douglas Fairbanks, Steffi Graf, Judy Garland, Che Guevara, Bob Hope, Thomas Hardy, Nichole Kidman, Henry Kissenger, Stan Laurel, Christopher Lee, Dean Martin, Robert Morley, Thomas Mann, Paul McCartney, Marilyn Munroe, Anton Mesmer, Bob Monkhouse, Michael Portillo, Salman Rushdie, Dorothy Sayers, Brooke Shields, Jackie Stewart, Stravinsky, Richard Strauss, John-Paul Sartre, Donald Trump, Queen Victoria, Venus Williams, Walt Whitman, John Wayne, Richard Wagner, W.B. Yeats.

Moon in Gemini

Joan Baez, Brigitte Bardot, Billy Connolly, Noel Coward, Edwina Curry, Doris Day, Kirk Douglas, Amelia Earhart, Sigmund Freud, Goldie Hawn, Buddy Holly, Anthony Armstrong Jones, Rudyard Kipling, Mussolini, Spike Milligan, Jack Nicklaus, Roy Orbison, Edith Piaf (the little bird), Claudia Schiffer, Omar Sharif, Brook Shields, Tina Turner.

Ascendant in Gemini

Neil Armstrong, Tony Blair, Michael Caine, Bob Dylan, Dante, Steffi Graf, Greta Garbo, Audrey Hepburn, Bob Hope, Henry Kissenger, Gregory Peck, George Peppard, Michelle Pfeiffer, Michael Stich, George Bernard Shaw.

 # CANCER

The symbol is that of the Crab. Cancer is the first Water Sign and is associated with creativity, caring, nurturing and the need for home and emotional security.

KEYWORDS: *Security, nurturing, moody, creativity mediumistic, personal.*

The study of History and our Ancestors is the key to all wisdom .
Jonathan Swift - Gulliver's Travels

Cancer

SUN IN CANCER

(Birthday between June 21st and July 22nd)

"Happiness is as a butterfly which, when pursued, is always beyond our grasp, but which if you will sit down quietly, may alight upon you."
Nathaniel Hawthorne

So, you have been blessed with a little Moon Child! As a parent you will need to know one simple thing - emotional well-being and emotional safety are the most important qualities for your child to acquire. Cancer is a mystical and reflective sign and being a Water sign, Cancerians are fluid, changeable, emotionally vulnerable and extremely sensitive. Just try connecting with the fluctuating monthly cycle of the Moon - New, Waxing, Full and Waning - and you will begin to understand the temperament of your Lunar Child. Cancer's symbol is the Mother and Child entwined and you find that your child, whether male or female, will naturally want to nurture and protect things which are young and vulnerable, whether it be their brothers and sisters, their toys, a plant, or perhaps their creative imaginations. Cancers are great propagators!

Your child may, from time to time, be in the process of gestating the fruits which grow readily from their intuitive and creative imaginations and will need at such times to withdraw into themselves, like the Crab under a rock. This sign abounds with original creativity and giving 'birth' comes naturally to your little Crab, whether it be a new idea or some project with which they are involved. Often, this will not come from an intellectual perspective, but from a deep sense of being connected to the magical secrets of life. Cancer is known as the 'midwife of the Zodiac'.

A Cancer child will display mood-swings from time to time - don't try to bring them out of these moods too quickly. Like the tides, these swings of mood take time to ebb and flow. Remember that the tides flush clean the sands over which they wash. Let your child process their feelings and you will see their sometimes round Moon faces light up again with a knowing, grateful glance. Sometimes it might appear to you that your child's nature is very like the ocean - unfathomable. Don't be alarmed at this, try to remember that Cancer the Crab can live on both land and sea and when they plunge into the fluid depths of their feelings, let them, for they will return with the all the wisdom and magic they have found there.

Cancer is a sign of great depth of feeling and is extremely sensitive and sentimental. You will find your Cancerian very tender and loving. They are children who tend to take things very personally, and like all the water signs, following an argument, tend to withdraw into a safe place nursing their wounds, real or imagined, which they retain in their very long memories. Picture the crab, who hides under a rock when security is threatened. This retentive side of their nature can be a

blessing and a curse, for like the crab, Cancer will hold onto an emotional experience (or a person) far longer than some of the less complicated signs, and thereby become caught or emotionally enmeshed in the memory of that experience. In these situations, learning to 'let go' will be an important lesson for your child, for, like the elephant, Cancerians never, ever, forget. Because of their wonderful memory and their special interest in history, Cancer has good recall of places and events which they often see in pictures. This makes them talented at creative writing or painting and they have a wonderful gift for telling stories, especially ones that appeal to the inner imagination of the child. Learn to listen during those special moments with your child.

Because Cancerians have a fascination with the past, don't be surprised when they relate dates in history or an event that has happened to the family which is connected to the past in some way or another. Cancer abounds with creative energy, but usually always with the emphasis on looking back. Michael Flatley, who has both Sun and Moon in Cancer, is a prime example of this characteristic - his powerfully evocative traditional dancing connects audiences to the music and dancing of his ancestors in Ireland.

Because of their maternal and nurturing qualities Cancerians need to mother something or someone. Like all the water signs, Cancer needs to be needed, so always remember to praise your child when they want to help you around the house and garden. Let them experiment in the kitchen and let your child 'mother' you occasionally, by making you a cup of tea or baking you a special cake. Cancer is the nourisher of the Zodiac. You will find the notorious 'crabby' side of their personality emerges if they are not getting enough emotional nourishment. This is when they get a bit clingy, but if you can see through the mask, and their tough outer shell, you can help them understand that not everybody appreciates this neediness, helping them develop in a positive way their independence and ability to stand alone whilst protecting their fragile and tender inner centre.

Cancer's association with the sign of the Mother means that your child will show much attachment and affinity to the parents very early on and will never be far away from their mother's or father's side, seeking closeness, assurance and parental support. However, it would be a good idea to encourage your child to develop a sense of independence and of doing things on their own occasionally. This teaches them about boundaries and discrimination which will make it easier to break the powerful bond that they have with the family when the time arrives for them to find a safe place for themselves in the outer World.

Because of Cancer's fascination with the past, you will find that your child may be an avid collector and right from an early age will have a shrewd eye for a bargain and will intuitively know the value of things because of their deep connection to the Earth's resources, its seasons and cycles. It also gives them a sense of emotional security knowing that the items they surround themselves with have a connection to the past as they have a positive horror of being cut-off, alone and feeling isolated from the flow of life. Cancer children love to have a little place in the family house which they can call 'Home' - their own special hideaway or den where they can play with that special toy or item to which they have become so attached. Although this may be a 'secret' place, you might get an invite there if you wait to be asked.

Moon

MOON IN CANCER

Stay at home and cultivate your own garden.

Voltaire

With the Moon placed in this magical, mystical sign, your child possesses a fluid, changeable, vulnerable and extremely sensitive nature. Just like the cycles of the Moon, to which your child will readily connect, be prepared for their mood swings and try to understand that they naturally connect to these changes in their personality and often can't understand why others around them react so vehemently. Try to remember that this is a sign that reacts immediately to those around them but needs time to process and then change their emotional responses. This 'out of phase' quality means that Cancer Moon can be immediately emotionally unsettled by subtle changes in the home, or in the disposition of those with whom they interact.

Cancer

It will be difficult to hide your real feelings from your Moon-Cancer child, as they pick up immediately whether you are feeling happy or sad. They will love to share feelings with you and love to be needed in this way, so show them your vulnerability and let them protect and nurture you for, after all, you do have a 'little Mother' on your hands whether you have a male or a female child.

Your Cancer Moon child may show signs of being possessive, this is because they need to be first in your affections and if you are someone who likes to be alone or needs a little space at times, this can seem a little suffocating - the mothering could become smothering. Give your Cancer Moon all the re-assurance they need and encourage them to do things alone occasionally and to be more emotionally self-sufficient. Then, you will be preparing them to approach life and the outside world in a more adult way which will be necessary for their survival as they grow older.

Cancer is the 'baby' of the Zodiac and needs all the loving, care and affection that you can find time for. Even when your child gets bigger, they will need and deeply appreciate their 'baby' being cared for. Sometimes you may see them regress into babyish behaviour when their feelings have been hurt or damaged by less sensitive souls, retreating into their shell, which could result in cravings for their favourite foods. Fresh baked bread, milky drinks and chocolate, indeed *all* foods connected to Mama are their favourites. The Cancer constitution can often be a bit sluggish, and is noted for fluid retention, so it is important to encourage your child to take regular exercise, getting out into the good fresh air. So watch their diet and help them to take a keen interest in keeping their bodies trim, fit and moving. Looking like the full moon is not the best physical expression of the sign!

Do watch out for the famous Cancerian side-step! Like the crab, when they need something or somebody, they will never approach you directly, like an Aries would. This is because they have a deep rooted fear of being rejected. You have to learn to read the signs and read

Ascendant

through the lines and quietly ask them exactly what they need, otherwise you could have to deal with *The Incredible Sulk* - that famous Cancerian sulking and whinging, or them just plain mooning about. Try to re-assure your lunar child that they are loved and explain that although you may not always be able to tend to their needs immediately, you will be there for them as soon as you can.

Cancer Moon has a deep connection to the past and those with this placement are noted for their retentive memories and recall. This can be both a blessing and a curse for, like the elephant, Cancer never forgets. This can build up resentment and you could have a very withdrawn and emotionally manipulative little crab on your hands. If this is allowed to accumulate, the crab's shell will thicken and your child will over-protect itself against the surrounding environment. In other words, hiding under the rock - *withdrawing* - will become more frequent. These are the danger signs for the parent of a Cancerian child who should try and instil the benefits of moving onwards following a set-back, and not wallowing in the muddy waters of old bad feelings. And do try to help them retain the good part of their impressive memory by telling or writing stories - perhaps acting, painting and performing. Cancer's highly coloured emotions, when used creatively, will be a joy to all those around who will reap the rewards of their deeply connected wisdom for these are truly the creative children of the Zodiac.

ASCENDANT IN CANCER

The glamour of childish days is upon me, my manhood is cast - down in the flood of remembrance. I weep like a child for the past.

D. H. Lawrence

With Cancer on the Ascendant your child should be encouraged to develop a fine and sophisticated attunement to their feeling nature. At the same time, they will need to learn to protect themselves from the harder aspects of life by finding a way of using their deeply sensitive nature rather than being overwhelmed by it. Many psychologists, carers and counsellors have this Ascendant. There is a high degree of creative force available to this Ascending sign. If their conceptual skills are highly developed, many Cancerians feel with some agitation that

they must bring forth or 'birth' something - a play, a composition or a painting. Being aware of their sometimes turbulent feelings, feelings which are often masked under the surface of a cool and collected exterior, will be of great assistance in mastering and channelling the feeling nature constructively. The Ascendant is a lot to do with how we start things, either a project or a relationship, and with this rising sign, there could be a tendency to be backwards in coming forwards. Nothing haunts the Cancerian heart as much as the fear of emotional failure, rejection or collapse. Thus, there may be a certain reticence and fear about approaching new ventures. Therefore your Cancer Ascendant child may approach situations and people sideways, like the crab - which can be very confusing for others, who will perhaps see such behaviour as manipulative and devious.

The symbolism behind this behavioural trait is simple - Cancer, above all the other signs, needs emotional reassurance, fears being rejected and does not 'boldly go into that dark night' of emotional risk-taking. It is as well to encourage the development of some strong boundaries around the self, protecting this extremely sensitive and

vulnerable Ascendant point. As Cancer is so deeply embedded in their instinctive response to life, it is important to develop a more grown up approach to life and situations enabling the creativity of this nurturing energy to be used effectively in the World. Your child will be acutely sensitive to the atmosphere in the home environment and to the feeling nature of the parents, particular the one who most adopts the maternal role. It is important to encourage this quality of caring and protection,

Ascendant

whether you have a male or female Cancerian. In adult life, this will equip them better to nurture a family, care for a business concern or for people or support a deeply felt cause. As this Ascendant energy matures, it could display the gift of 'the common touch' knowing instinctively what will be popular and therefore highly desirable in the market place which will stand them in good stead in the field of business matters.

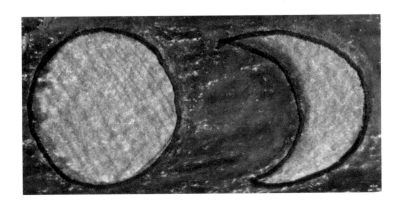

FAMOUS CANCERIANS

Sun in Cancer

Giorgio Armani, Louis Armstrong, Richard Branson, Richard Bach, Camilla Parker-Bowles, Princess Diana, Kathy Bates, Tom Cruise, Barbara Cartland, Pierre Cardin, William Defoe, Jacques Delors, Harrison Ford, Adam Faith, Michael Flatley, Tom Hanks, Woody Guthrie, Lena Horne, Ernest Hemmingway, Rider Haggard, Lord Kitchener, Helen Keller, Sue Lawley, Johanthan Miller, Gustav Mahler, Lord Mountbatten, George Orwell, Mervyn Peake, Emmeline Pankhurst, Marcel Proust, Rembrant, Elisabeth Kubler-Ross, Ken Russell, Diana Rigg, Richard Rogers, Ginger Rogers, George Sand, Tom Stoppard, Meryl Streep, Carlos Santana, Ringo Starr, Sylvester Stallone, Donald Sutherland, John Anthony West, Colin Wilson, Prince William, Robin Williams.

Moon in Cancer

Giorgio Armani, Anastasia, Charles Baudelaire, Camilla Parker- Bowles, Harrison Ford, Aretha Franklin, Andre Gide, Charlton Heston, Julio Inglesis, Janis Joplin, Olivia Newton John, Liza Minnelli, Mary Tyler Moore, Thomas Mann, Tatum O'Neal, Giacomo Puccini, Paul Simon, Stavinsky, Steve Winwood, Prince William.

Ascendant in Cancer

Alfred Adler, Robert Assagioli, Cilla Black, Cher, Albert Einstein, David Frost, Ian Fleming, Judy Garland, Glenda Jackson, Rudyard Kipling, Rimsky Korsakov, George Michael, Ryan O'Neal, Arnold Schwarzenegger, Steven Spielberg, John Travolta.

LEO

The symbol is the Male Lion's Mane. Leo is the second Fire Sign, representing power and constancy, the fire of the heart and the steady controlled fire of affection.

KEYWORDS: *Self-expression, creative, courageous, commanding, noble.*

Your heart is free - have the courage to follow it.

William Wallace (*Braveheart*)

Leo

SUN IN LEO

(Birthday between July 21st and August 23rd)

Like the Lion, Leo's noble symbol, your Leo child will love to be the centre of attention and shine brightly at everything they do. The Sun, the astrological ruler of this sign, lies at the centre of our Solar System, so it will be impossible to remain unaware of your child's 'royal' and central presence. Their available energy, which also commands attention, is boundless, as is their 'pride of place' at the centre of whatever they do. Leo children (and of course adults!) display an air of authority and demand to be noticed and appreciated everywhere they go, unless your little Lion has a more subdued Moon or Ascendant sign.

As a parent, make sure that your Leo child is allowed to be the King or Queen sometimes, for like all the fire signs, Leo most of all needs (and often demands) this kind of attention. Somehow you won't mind giving it to them either, for they are warm-hearted and are often generous to a fault. Like their ruler the Sun, the brightest star in the heavens, they will strive to shine and to convey that sunshine into your lives and to those around them. Leos, at their best, are fun to be around. They can also be exhausting and demanding, this being the sign associated with the prima donna and the maestro!

To deliver their best qualities, Leos often need an audience. With their strong sense of dramatic flair, they have a natural creativity and sense of drama and theatre. Perhaps it would be as well to encourage your Leo child to join the local theatre group where they can naturally be noticed. Eitherway, your little Leo will one day need a commanding position on life's stage where they can act out in a highly dramatic way the role of hero or heroine that they romantically carry within themselves.

Even if you have one of the more shy and introverted little Lions, try to encourage them to express this side of their nature and open-up their generous hearts from time to time, taking the lead or centre-stage sometimes, and they will be much happier. This child is a natural leader and manager, and Leos have a intrinsic ability to inspire and enthuse the more timid souls around them with their faith in life and their warm hearts. Never restrict your child's generosity nor their creative spirit, for if this is rejected or misunderstood, then you will have a very sad and depressed little Lion indeed. Cats loved to be stroked and to hold pride of place.

Leo has an almighty temper, so be prepared for the famous Leo roar. Stand well out of the line of fire and let them bellow. They will calm down just as soon as you stroke their manes and will once more purr if you tell them what beautiful 'pussycats' they are. More than any other

sign in the Zodiac, Leo loves to be loved and is often in love with life itself. This can turn into egotism, which is difficult for others who do not understand the quality of loving the *self* so easily displayed by this sign. Mick Jagger of Rolling Stones fame is a Leo and his performance on stage is often like that of the roaring lion as he proudly struts around the stage in front of thousands of adoring fans.

Leo is the fixed fire sign and like all the other fire signs can have a delightful child-like quality. As such, Leo's approach to life is often that of an innocent child, ready for a lot of excitement and surprise. When their enthusiasm fails to inspire or connect with those around them then there's the tension of the *prima donna* failing to connect to their audience and sparks can fly! But Leo is highly intuitive and often their hunches can turn an idea into a great vision if they can actualise and ground that vision into a reality. Try to encourage your sometimes over-exuberant and precocious little Leo to be as practical as possible with their creativity.

Because they often believe and naturally expect that the World revolves around them, they can seem self-centred and self-absorbed, but this is because instinctively Leo knows that to find their own centre, which is their task and their birthright, they need to be self aware and sometimes egocentric. The World is a difficult place and to succeed only a total belief in one's *self* will realise the near impossible ambitions that a Leo will take on board. Because of this, Leo can often

seem somewhat arrogant, pompous, bombastic and thick skinned to those more delicate souls around them. One of the most important lessons you can teach your Leo is to turn down their pride control button, and teach them to give praise and value to those folk who seem less significant, but who often have the humility and the quiet assistance to help them onto their throne - where they naturally belong, of course! You can see these traits in such Leos as Napoleon Bonaparte (Sun in Leo), Winston Churchill and Maggie Thatcher (both Moon in Leo).

You will experience a deep loyalty in your Leo child and because they are a fixed fire sign, an inability to compromise about certain matters. This is because the fixed signs often experience life as either black or white. Neutral grey is not at all a Leo colour, for they usually harbour strong opinions. Try to encourage your child to be more flexible and tolerant not only with themselves, but with others. Life will then become easier for everyone.

When the Sun is shining on Leo anything is possible, and life is there to be led to the full. Deep in the heart of every Leo, regardless of their exterior circumstances or their age, is the belief that to attain divinity one must first become childlike, innocent, carefree and joyful, for this will lead humanity out of its darkness and into the light. The greatest gift you can provide your Leo infant is the vehicle to achieve this, for then the gift they can bring to the World is to ascend through the ranks with an understanding, generous and compassionate heart.

Moon

MOON IN LEO

You can't have too much of a good thing.

Mae West

Well, my oh my, haven't you got a little show-off on you hands with your little Leo! You will learn very quickly that your Leo Moon child is warm, outgoing, self-centred, dramatic and lucky. They seem to have it all in terms of sheer 'chutzpah'. No one can beat a Leo Moon for personality and dramatic impact. Anything is possible with your Leo Moon, so light the touch paper and watch out. Life is there to explore

and this Moon positively needs to be encouraged to do just that. Seasonally, Leo is the time of high summer, when the plants in the garden compete for the available intensity of light and the flowers are performing and competing to display their brilliant yellows, reds and oranges. All these flowers need pride of place and if any other flowers try to peep through or hog the limelight, they soon get shoved off stage. This gives a good

feel as to the character of your Leo, Sun or Moon. But Moon Leos are more reflective, and will analyse and dissect their dramatic experiences afterwards, thus giving them more self-knowledge and consequently more sensitivity to those around them. Leo Moon is more at home and naturally relaxed about it's creativity and not as compulsively driven as perhaps a Leo Sun placement.

But if your Leo Moon is not given the opportunity to shine and be noticed and they think that others are getting too much of the spotlight, they will be very sad little 'pussycats' indeed. Therefore, always give them an opportunity to be heard or seen, preferably to stand in the spotlight. This child badly needs an audience to bounce off, not because they think of it as a duty or chore, but because they need it with all their heart. Your child will love to dress up, as Leo Moon loves finery and good clothes and will readily act out the romantic heroes and heroines that they dream about or read about in story books - anything that connects them to the colour, pomp and romanticism of King Arthur's Court and the Knights of the Round Table. Give them a bedroom full of books or videos with such heroic stories.

Boasting and bragging had a very bad press in the repressive culture of post-Victorian Britain, yet with Leo energy, justified self-aggrandisement should be actively encouraged by a parent, teacher or relative. You will find your Leo child extremely loyal and they will display a generosity of spirit that will touch your heart. Remember the Lion in the Wizard of Oz, his journey was to find his heart and his courage. Under the apparent shining armour of your playful Leo Moon lies a deep sense of vulnerability which needs constant praise and re-assurance.

Leo is always trying to find that unique special self through the joy of their creativity. They will want to believe in those fairy stories and myths where Kings and Queens, magicians and the Fairy Queen herself save the hero or heroine from the wicked witch of the wood or the monsters who lurk in the bushes. The Leo 'monster' is often the fear of failure and hurt pride. Even when your Leo Moon gets a little older, always remember their little 'child', for they will always have the ability to connect you to your 'inner child' who knows how to play and have fun inspite of those boring realities that have to be faced each day. Party on, parents!

Ascendant

ASCENDANT IN LEO

I cast my own warmth around me and it is reflected in others.

Anais Nin

Like the Lion, their symbol, your child with a Leo Ascendant should be proudly encouraged to develop a sense of unique specialness in their journey through life. They will need to develop a sense of their own power and naturally seek to lead and be in command of whatever they choose to do in life. Prince Charles has Leo rising, the sign of Kings and Queens, and sometimes with this Ascendant, your child will expect to

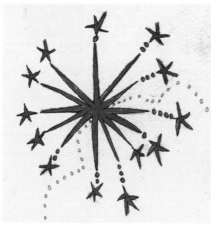

be treated like Royalty, which can be both disturbing and unrealistic to those with whom they come into contact. They should be encouraged to make an effort to earn the desired respect and status rather than getting angry if the power and the glory are not bestowed on them immediately without having to work for it. Leo tantrums need care in this area - crushing the spirit is not a solution and may permanently damage your child's self-confidence. Instead, aid your child in finding a vital and creative outlet for their deep sense of dignity, authority and self worth - let them find that which they are good at - then they will shine and find their own unique sense of power. They need to feel that they are experts or specialists or just plain good at something! And just as important, need to be *seen* being good at something.

Children with this Ascendant often have a powerful and commanding presence which demands attention and should be directed into professions that give them outlet to display these qualities to the full. Goldie Hawn and Mae West are delightful examples of the Leo Ascendant type. Actor, media 'star', working with children, managers, the company leader, anywhere where they can find a forum for their Kingly/Queenly bearing and where they can be seen and allowed to shine like the Stars they are.

FAMOUS LEOS

Sun in Leo

The Queen Mother, Princess Margaret, Princess Anne, Neil Armstrong, Conrad Aitkin, Lucille Ball, Madame Blavatsky, Kate Bush, Napoleon Bonaparte, John Logie Baird, Bill Clinton, Zelda Fitzgerald, Fidel Castro, Coco Chanel, Claude Debussy, Alexandra Dumas, Amelia Earhart, Henry Ford, Sir Alexander Fleming, Whitney Houston, Ted Hughes, Dustin Hoffman, Alfred Hitchcock, Mata Hari, C.G. Jung, Mick Jagger, Jackie Kennedy, Mark Knopfler, Stanley Kurbrick, Lawrence of Arabia, Yves St. Laurent, Bernard Levin, Steve Martin, George Melly, Benito Mussolini, Madonna, Peter O'Toole, Beatrix Potter, Robert De Niro, Robert Redford, Rasputin, Alan Shearer, George Bernard Shaw, Percy Bysshe Shelley, Arnold Schwarzenegger, Alfred Lord Tennyson, Mae West, Terry Wogan.

Moon in Leo

Queen Elizabeth II, Prince Phillip, Winston Churchill, John Foster Dulles, Marlene Dietrich, Tom Cruise, Clint Eastwood, Jane Fonda, Tom Hanks, George Michael, Paul McCartney, Dolly Parton, Ringo Starr, Barbara Streisand, Maggie Thatcher, Venus Williams, Oscar Wilde.

Ascendant in Leo

Prince Charles, Prince Andrew, Camilla Parker Bowles, Mohammed Ali, Anastasia, Paddy Ashdown, Richard Branson, Glen Close, Aleister Crowley, Edwina Currie, Alexandra Dumas, Durer, Galileo, Indira Ghandi, Peter Gabriel, Jeremy Irons, Elton John, Marilyn Monroe, Steve Martin, Ian McShane, Jack Nicholson, Luciano Pavarotti, Vanessa Redgrave.

♍ VIRGO ♍

The symbol is that of the Corn Maiden. Virgo is the second Earth Sign and the sixth Sign of the Zodiac and represents the gathering of the harvest after the work has been well prepared and completed.

KEYWORDS: *Discriminating, reserved, skilled, practical, understated.*

Perform small tasks with great love.

Anonymous

Virgo

SUN IN VIRGO

(Birthday between August 23rd and September 23rd)

Whether you have the joy of either a male or female Virgo child, there will be something very demure and graceful about this mutable Earth sign. Virgo is the sign of the harvest and Virgo knows right from a very early age that whatever you sow into your life will be rewarded or harvested if you put time and effort into developing your talents to the full. There is an extremely adult head on your little Virgo's shoulders and they instinctively know, like their symbol of the Virgin Maiden with the sheaves of grain in her hands after the harvest, that true wisdom is gleaned only in the field of real hands-on experience. Reserved and practical, Virgo is the most realistic sign of the Zodiac and has a deep respect for the slogan *'if a job is worth doing, it's worth doing well'*.

You will notice very early the scrupulous perfectionist streak in your child. They could be quite a fusspot, noticing details that others would not find important or relevant, even becoming quite anxious if something isn't quite as it should be. Remember that this is because they like to be seen as discriminating, and of doing things the right way. Virgos need praise and gratitude for attending to all those little things that others find unimportant - for they uphold and practice the 'art of the small' and usually excel at anything that requires detailed and painstaking accuracy. Many precision engineers, artists and craftspeople have this sign prominent in their charts, and of all the signs, Virgo is the most discriminating, and requires that things are done properly. Overdone, this trait produces the fusspot and the worrier.

Sometimes you may find that your Virgo child finds it difficult to just play. They would much rather be helping you around the house and doing grown up jobs. Do try to ensure that they do play sometimes, just for the fun of it and just for themselves occasionally.

At the heart of most Virgos is the desire to be of service, to be helpful and get involved in the everyday rituals of life and particularly those which belong in the home. They will often love to help Mum and Dad with all the household chores and get lots of praise for doing so (well who wouldn't just relish a child like this?). This is the sign of the harvest and right from the beginning you will be impressed with the increased bounty delivered by your Virgo, and the helpfulness and intelligence of your Mercury ruled Earth child.

The word virgin, associated with the sign of Virgo, literally means, 'respect my separateness' and the most famous Virgo of them all, Greta Garbo whose famous expression "I want to be alone" could also apply to your child from time to time. Often extremely sensitive and highly strung, Virgoans need time alone to 'clean out' and rest their extremely sensitive physical and emotional systems. Because Virgo is ruled by the mind planet Mercury, you will find that they are forever on the move, seeking knowledge and asking questions "How does this work, Daddy" and "Show me how to work this, Mummy".

The sign Virgo also rules the healthy functioning of the body, so paying attention to their daily routine and habit patterns can help to alleviate or heal their extremely sensitive systems. Their tendency to worry and fuss can build up tension in the body which can lead to hypersensitivity and poor health. There is often an issue surrounding food with this sign, typified by the model Twiggy (Sun in Virgo), who, in the 60's, set a trend for models who were thin and malnourished. As a parent try to ensure they get enough food, plenty of rest, fresh air and regular exercise. This will help to build up their resistance to illness and aid the functioning of their bodies. To grow into strong fit adults, Virgoans need to be able to understand and connect to the rhythms and

 cycles of their physical body. It is also important for you to train your young Virgo to listen to the wisdom of what their body is telling them and treat it accordingly. It is not really surprising, therefore, that some of our finest

doctors, carers, healers and fitness instructors have this sign strong in their horoscope.

But whatever type of profession or vocation a Virgo ultimately chooses, it will be good if you can provide maximum access to books and learning. Virgo admires and respects the written word and they will adore browsing around bookshops. They will be very impressed by a well crafted and well written story and will delight in well chosen words, which will be like music to their ears. It would be a good idea to build a book-shelf for them in their nursery at an early age, even before they have their own room, as this will probably be a very special place for them. Handling and looking at books which convey the knowledge they seek, and then to make use of in their future lives, will delight your child. Even reference books and DIY books will be eagerly consumed. Virgos are seekers of knowledge, not just for the fun of it, like their Mercury-ruled cousin Gemini, but because knowledge may be applied for the good of the individual and Society, used to develop and perfect skills.

Deep in the heart of most Virgos is the belief that potentials should be used and not wasted - Virgo abhors waste - waste of resources and a waste of a life. Some of the best Virgos you will ever meet reclaim scrap materials or recycle other people's junk. Virgo is the "cosmic cleaner" of the Zodiac. They are drawn to work towards the optimum use of the gifts and talents that have been bestowed upon them.  Therefore, many are drawn towards a psychology profession or into teaching. The spiritual, esoteric and holistic healing arts are also heavily populated with this sign. Virgo is also the analyst and you will most probably find that every sentence begins with the word "why?" because inquisitive Virgo has a need to know everything. Let your little one know that you think they are knowledgeable and try not to criticise them for sometimes being 'little know-alls'. Their insatiable thirst for knowledge will help them develop their potentially brilliant minds. The word *virtuoso* is connected to this sign, and means a person with special knowledge and skilled in the application of their art. All Virgo children aspire to becoming *virtuosi* in some form or another.

You can see this attention to detail in developing of their skills in such famous people as Sean Connery and Richard Gere (Sun Virgo), Shirley Maclaine and the late Sir Laurence Olivier (Moon Virgo). These folk are all craftspeople, delicately honing a fine edge onto their increasing skills and talents. Whatever Virgo does it likes to do well and to the best of their ability and if you can guide them along in life to do just that, you will have a very appreciative and healthy little Virgo on your hands indeed. Make sure you guide and help your child to find

Sun

the right work or profession. Skills need to be *vocational* for a Virgo and your child should be encouraged to develop the tools of their trade or profession in whatever they want to do in life with great dedication and attention to detail. However trivial you may think the task, keep on piling on the encouragement. The worst that can go wrong is that your little Virgo exhausts their bodies by trying too hard, fretting and becoming obsessed with the task in hand. Unfortunately, this can occur over some small detail which the more "thick skinned" signs would not even notice. Please try not to become irritated at this less than perfect attempt to master a small task, but equally do not offer to help unless asked into the 'workshop' of your budding perfectionist!

Virgo has the reputation of spotting an error or a mistake at long distance. As a Virgo friend of mine once said about men, "I can spot dandruff on his jacket at five hundred paces", so keen is their perfectionists eye. Of course, taken to excess this trait may mean that the objects underneath life's 'dandruff' become ignored, leading to a different expression, which must have originated for application to Virgos, that they 'can't see the wood for the trees'. Too much attention to the small detail can sometimes leave this sign strangely unable to capture or enjoy the bigger, overall picture.

The Virgoan constitution is essentially simple. To remain healthy, regular rituals and routines, which revolve around healthy living, will ensure that good health becomes the norm. Remember that monks and nuns wear habits, and the origin of the sign Virgo stems from the Kore of ancient Sumeria, who were temple priestesses. Connection to the rituals and habits associated with the body and it's comfort should be encouraged at every stage of a Virgo child's daily development.

Virgo is the sixth sign of the Zodiac and often they have a "sixth sense" about animals and will often love and pay special attention to pets. Perhaps they will ask you for a pet and will then ask to look after it. They will delight in grooming pets and often show special affinity with animals so that working with animals becomes a sought after

career option. Many vets have a strong Virgo emphasis in their horoscopes. Right from birth Virgoans are in touch with that "wise" animal within which can become their special guide through life - you might just hear them talking to it!

Virgo

Deep in the heart of this helpful and thoughtful 'little adult', who is often dying to be your little helper and servant, is the sensitive and tender heart of the dreamer of dreams and the poet, who seeks perfection through service, and whose poetry is skill at a craft. Here, the link with their opposite sign of Pisces becomes apparent.

MOON IN VIRGO

She's so industrious, when she has nothing to do, she sits and knits her brows.

Anon

You may notice that a child with the Moon in the sign of Virgo will give off an air of having been here before, and appear to know quite a lot about life. In fact you may feel like you are the child and they are the adult. This Moon position confers a great need to assist and be of service in the domestic arena which, however dull it may be to us lesser folk, intrigues them enough to develop skills in these areas. But remember, in your surprise and delight, to lavish praise and encouragement on your child, and remember too that routine in the home will actually help to keep them happy and healthy children. Moon Virgo can become quite 'nervy' and anxious if the domestic order isn't there, or if the house gets into disorder. The rituals and habits of everyday life - washing, shopping, cleaning, gardening - offer security through work and routine, all of which appeals to the Moon Virgo ethic.

Because Virgo is an Earth sign, and the Moon relates to the stomach, it is also important that eating is somehow ritualised, and the Moon placed here suggests attention on detail in nourishing your child. The ritual of preparing food whilst being aware of what food does to the system will appeal to your budding 'little chemist'. Some children will benefit from a special diet, or have food allergies, and an alert parent

Moon

needs to spot what is going on before it becomes a problem. Health is a paramount consideration for this position, and the worst scenario is that chaotic domestic life coupled with mealtimes being disrupted will lead to them being thrown off balance - a torture to such a sensitive Moon position. Because their antennae are constantly on alert, missing nothing about what is going on in the immediate environment, your little Virgo may get overwhelmed and exhausted, occasionally needing to be alone for a while. Like the opposite sign of Pisces, space should be available in the day for recharging the batteries.

Happily, one can always reason with a child who has Moon (or Sun) here and they will understand from an early age that your motives are good and why you want your little angel to go to bed, or rest. You will probably never have to ask that they tidy their room, although sometimes you can meet a Virgoan adult who has completely lost the ability to maintain order in their domestic life or in their vocation, and has focused all this energy into a passionate hobby, like clock mending,

marquetry or some other devotional activity which may demand inordinate amounts of patience.

If you become irritated when your 'little know-all' tells you that the way you clean the bath could be done better, then remember this - your child will be self-sufficient and auto-nomous way before most and will pull their weight in the home so that you can share the chores. Isn't that wonderful? However, you may need to urge them to indulge in playful activities from time to time. Virgo can sometimes be so heavy-heavy serious as to make domestic activities assume too much importance. To avoid this, praise their helpfulness, and play down the importance of any failures over tiny details, responding adult-to-adult whenever possible. Then your Moon Virgo will learn to work hard and to play hard. And happy little Virgos are such pleasant folk to have around.

Virgo

ASCENDANT IN VIRGO

An opportunity to serve - that's all I ask.

Gordon Brown - Virgo Ascendant

Virgo rising gives a clue that your child needs to be of service in some way. As a parent, you should try and spot the tools and equipment needed for your child to develop the skills they will need. Perhaps it will be experiences they will need, but you need to be on the ball and recognise this need early on. Remember that virtuosi musicians start very early on, often developing their skills before the age of five. Not all of these are Virgos, of course, but you would be surprised at how many top musicians, artists and composers have this sign emphasised in their horoscope. Mozart who had this Ascendant lived a fairly chaotic life, but his musical scores where written immaculately with no messy corrections, in fact they were perfected works of art in their own right, immediately they came off the composer's pen.

There will be a vital need to understand and relate to the body, issues relating to purity and cleanliness, and a need to discover the sanctity of service to others. Virgo rising can become quite ill at ease if these needs are not met. Developing the skills of discrimination, reliability, punctuality should be encouraged from an early age, in order to develop any craft or skill to which they are drawn. This Ascending sign is often cautious, with a reserve and dignity which can sometimes lead to lost chances through fear of taking risks or not getting it right first time around. Help your child to recognise the pros and cons of each decision they need to take, and then to list them. This may be a painstaking and drawn out act, but you will discover that, even while young, they are very able to articulate the factors involved, even amazing you with their powers of observation and discrimination.

Obsessiveness can arise if children with Virgo rising are allowed to become too reclusive, particularly if the World does not live up to their standards of perfection. Howard Hughes (Virgo Ascendant) remains perhaps the best example of this trait, although Peter Sellers was also noted for obsessive behaviour. A good social interaction should be encouraged, with attention to the arts and crafts. When Virgo stops striving for whatever perfection they seek, then watch out, for this Ascendant needs to seek work and service, or grumpiness may ensue. Mozart was impossible to be near when he was not simultaneously at work on three or four masterpieces, although each would emerge as 'complete perfection' and radiate harmony.

Virgo is an earth sign. A parent needs to recognise that practical solutions will always be sought by a child who has this Ascendant. Because Mercury is the ruler of the sign, these solutions will be articulated clearly and precisely. There may be a strongly critical streak which may be irritating for parents and their friends to accept. But listen to what is said, and more than likely your child will display that quality sometimes difficult to find in the market place today - good old common sense.

FAMOUS VIRGOANS
Sun in Virgo

Leonard Bernstein, Yasser Arafat, Ingrid Bergman, Jaqueline Bisset, Lord George Brown, Shirley Conran, Agatha Christie, Maurice Chevalier, Claudette Colbert, Anne Diamond, Antonio Fraser, Stephen Fry, Henry Ford II, Greta Garbo, Barry Gibb, Goethe, Richard Gere, Larry Hagman, Gustave Holst, Buddy Holly, Denis Healey, Christopher Isherwood, Jeremy Irons, Julio Inglesias, Samuel Johnson, Lyndon B. Johnson, Louis XIV, Sophie Loren, Raymond Massey, Maria Montessori, Bob Newhart, Jesse Owens, Dorothy Parker, J.B. Priestley, Jimmie Rogers, Peter Sellers, Claudia Schiffer, Mother Teresa, Raquel Welch, Fay Weldon, H.G. Wells.

Moon in Virgo

The Dalai Lama, Princess Anne, Alexander Graham Bell, Richard Branson(Virgin), Richard Burton, Jodie Foster, Andy Gibb, Dustin Hoffman, Lyndon B Johnson, John F. Kennedy, Lulu, Madonna, Shirley McClaine, Jack Nicholson, Sir Lawrence Olivier Michelle Pfeiffer, Robert Redford, Vanessa Redgrave, Count Tolstoy, John Travolta.

Virgo

Virgo Ascendant

Jane Austen, Mary Astor, Elizabeth Barrett Browning, Charles Baudelaire, Charlotte Bronte, Kathy Bates, Kevin Costner, Walt Disney, Marlene Dietrich, Placido Domingo, Howard Hughes, Tom Hanks, Hugh Hefner, Ernest Hemmingway, Derek Jacobi, Olivia Newton John, Wolfgang Amadeus Mozart, George Melly, Thomas Mann, Roy Orbison, Raphael, Peter Sellers, Frank Sinatra, Igor Stravinsky, Cybil Shepherd, Brooke Shields, Paul Simon, Oscar Wilde.

Lavender rising. The ancient myths of the Corn Goddess are linked to the astrological sign of Virgo. This is here exemplified by the author, who has Virgo rising on her Ascendant, while on holiday in France.

LIBRA

The symbol or glyph is that of the Scales, representing balance and harmony. Librans find this in the sphere of relationships. Libra is the second Air Sign, and has the only glyph that is neither animal nor human.

KEYWORDS: *Justice, negotiation, compromise, strategy, arbitrators, peace-makers, civilised.*

May a Star shine upon the hour of our meeting .

J.R.Tolkien - The Hobbit

Libra

SUN IN LIBRA
(Birthday between 23rd September and 22nd November)

If your child was born with the Sun passing through the sign of Libra, then you definitely have one of the great charmers of the Zodiac in your midst. Venus, the planet of love, beauty, pleasure and harmony, rules supreme in this most civilised of signs. You will notice very early, how your little Libra tries to balance and weigh themselves against others, hence the Libran reputation and indeed pre-occupation with the art of right relationship.

They know instinctively how to charm the birds right out of the trees and have a natural desire to be diplomatic and co-operative, recognising immediately when there is conflict or discord in their environment. Conflict and discord will greatly upset their applecart if it wobbles their acute sense of balance. Librans are the peacemakers of the Zodiac and have a natural desire to be diplomatic and co-operative. Always remember that they are an Air sign, and like the element of air, they possess a cool and sometimes detached temperament. This enables them to keep themselves at a distance and view life from afar, therefore not getting too wrapped up in messy emotional swamplands which may be fine for the Water signs but not at all comfortable for the Air signs. Libra prefers the sharp, cutting edge of the mind with which to deal with relationship or negotiating issues.

You will find that your Libra child is a good strategist and loves the challenge of duelling and debating with you and others over issues that are important to them. Idealistic and romantic Librans prefer to dwell in an 'ivory tower' of beautiful experiences and they abhor coarseness or ugliness, in fact any form of discord makes them feel ill-tempered. Librans have artistic natures and a good balanced eye for colour and design, so try to give them an arena in the home where they can assist you with arranging the furniture, choosing a colour scheme or placing a well-loved picture in just the right spot.

Very soon, you will notice that your Libran child likes to arbitrate within the atmosphere of the home. They make wonderful referees because of this and are acutely sensitive to unpleasant atmospheres which interfere with their keen sense of equilibrium. With Venus their ruler, Librans are famous for their beauty and their even-handed, graceful demeanour. This applies to both sexes. Roger Moore, who portrayed James Bond, brought the quality of charm and grace to the part with the emphasise on lightness of touch. Even in the most difficult situations, you will see your Libra child displaying the ability

to act in a very civilised way, very rarely losing their cool and almost always trying to see the other persons point of view.

Remember, this is an Air sign and Librans needs to debate and discuss issues, as well as enjoy the finer things in life. Librans are refined folk and do not like raw instinctual behaviour; note that the glyph of the sign, as for all the Air signs, is not of an animal which represents the basic side of our natures. They prefer to rest their eyes on everything that is beautiful and harmonious. Coarse behaviour or language offends them. Even in a heated argument, your little Libra will rarely lose their charm and decorum. Maggie Thatcher (Sun in Libra) has this quality par excellence as does Bill Clinton (Libra Ascendant). They display grace, diplomacy and *entente cordiale* in the face of many adversaries. Libra will always try to find the middle ground in a situation, and their concern for justice always seems to lead them into the arena of debate and discussion. This is why many of them are drawn eventually into the field of politics and law.

Always try too give your child an arena where they can exercise their diplomatic skills and make sure they get lots of mental stimuli. Air signs desperately need to communicate, so they can weigh and balance those Libra scales. Because of their desire for equality and harmony, their pleasing natures can sometimes appear a little hypocritical to the more confrontational types. Some of our greatest strategists in battle have this sign in their horoscopes - Alexandra the Great (Sun in Libra), Lord Nelson and Winston Churchill (Libra Ascendant).

Do make sure that your Libra child gets a good education and a chance to exercise their debating skills and fine intellect to the full. This could eventually lead them to become negotiators, lawyers, diplomats, counsellors or presenters, in any walk of life. Many Librans become involved in personnel recruitment or spokespersons and negotiators for big organisations. With their love of beauty and harmony, they are attracted to the fields of art and music. Beauty fascinates and enchants them, and many become models, make up artists and set designers. On this point, it is as well to have a mirror in

your child's bedroom. This sign is associated with the Goddess Aphrodite and she was known to be always before her mirror. You will notice that your child takes a keen interest in their personal appearance and in the choosing of a colour co-ordinated wardrobe. So take delight in their vanity, as it is part of their nature.

Help your Libra child not to be 'all things to all people' in their search for peace, because if 'peace at any price' is their motto, it can create a rather superficial harmony, rather than a natural balance. If Libra compromises too much, it could lead to emotional repression, ill health and create difficulties and tensions in relationships. Try to encourage your Libra to value the art of a little robust confrontation, realising that sometimes it is healthier and cleaner to honestly confront unpleasantness and difficult situations, thereby releasing anger and discord so that true balance can be restored. Then your little Libra will learn that they are truly the personal and social peacemakers and for a moment in time, their scales will be perfectly balanced.

Moon

MOON IN LIBRA

When faced with life's little challenges, dither ye not and make your flipping mind up.

Alan Titchmarsh (7th house Sun)

Haven't you noticed how your Libra child has perfect manners and manages to do and say just the right things in difficult situations? You have one of the seductive charmers of the Zodiac in your family. Right from the start you will notice that your Libra Moon child could be over-sensitive and over-adaptive to the needs of everyone around them, such is their acute sensitivity to creating harmony and balance in their surroundings. This Moon position needs and indeed craves relationship and their friends will be extremely important to them. Because this is

the sign of partnership, your Libra child will need to have someone to play with and interact with - your child is definitely not a loner and will probably be quite social and an eager party-goer. One of the interpretations of the glyph for Libra is the Sun just setting over the horizon and, at sunset time, around 6-7pm, we are usually ready to socialise and get together with our friends - even calling this time 'happy hour'. Libra is such a social sign, positively craving being with others to exchange ideas and have fun. You will find that Libra Moon needs desperately to be liked by everyone and this can lead them to attempt to be all things to all men. Although over-accommodation to other's wishes is their natural way, try to encourage your Libra child to stand up for themselves when important issues are at stake, thereby creating or setting up a natural balance with others.

Try not to be too impatient with Libra when you see them struggling to make an important decision. They literally can see two sides of the story and always try to accommodate the other persons viewpoint. Rushing them into making up their minds will make them dither and upset their acute sense of balance and fair play. Helping them realise that sometimes you cannot please everybody and occasionally 'sticking to your guns' and making a clean choice about something is just as noble as trying to strike a compromise. For like Humpty Dumpty, if they sit on the fence too long, they are bound to fall off feeling hurt and resentful because they haven't stood up for their own principles.

Your Libra Moon child will usually have more than their fair share of good looks. Famous Libran Brigitte Bardot was born under the Libra Star and her professional life focused on her beautiful sex appeal and coquettish charm. Make sure that they have their own personal mirror as in the myths Venus was a vain goddess, always in front her mirror. You'll find a healthy streak of vanity in your Libra Moon child so encourage them to take an interest in their appearance. In fact you will want to do this for your Venus male or female child because they are so beautiful. They will love their food too, but if the scales are not balanced and their emotions out of harmony there could be signs of over-eating and excess. Money too is important to this Moon. Not because of the power it brings, but because this sign, more  than any other, loves the beautiful things of life which pleases their aesthetic eye and money enables them to buy the beautiful objects which give them so much pleasure. And pleasure and beauty is what Librans naturally seek.

You will see a definite artistic streak in your child, perhaps expressed through music, singing or an interest in design. Walt Disney (Moon in Libra) was an adept artist, designer and master in combining film with music, and his work remains justifiably famous. Libra's acute sense of colour combinations and balance makes them fine candidates for a profession in interior design or fashion. Playing a Musical instrument could be another artistic option for Libra - their finely balanced ear for a good tune will enable them to perform well in this activity.

Ascendant

ASCENDANT IN LIBRA

The ability to compromise is what makes a man noble.

Robert the Bruce of Scotland

If your child has a Libra Ascendant, life should be approached with the view to developing and striving for equality and harmony in all areas of their life. This Ascendant searches for fairness - the perfect balance in life, looking for that which is harmonious and pleasing. Weighing and balancing their value systems against others value systems will be an important lesson for this Ascendant to learn as they jostle so desperately to find the middle ground in all their dealings with

others. Sitting on the fence when important decisions are to be made will prove very difficult for this Ascendant, so making choices based on a sound value system will prove very beneficial and affective to Libra rising. To do this, they need a good education where they can utilise their mind and exercise their fine debating skills to the full.

Sometimes the ability to see both sides of the story could be crippling to your Libra child, so try to encourage them not to dither and to take the full consequences for their decisions and actions. True balance can only come from a position of equal strength tempered with consideration. Imbalance leads to the over-sweet 'niceness' sometimes attributed to Libra or to the very discord that the sign actively tries to avoid. Liz Taylor has a Libran Ascendant and her life path lesson has encompassed a strong need to relate and balance her power with that of her many husbands. Her Venus placed in the opposite confrontational sign of Aries provides one clue to her challenging behaviour in this arena of her life.

'Lazy Libra' could sometimes be applied to this Ascending sign. Princess Anne's (Libran Ascendant) school report once said, 'economy of effort is her watchword' - a phrase itself a Libran master-stroke of tact and diplomacy. However, she continues to champion good causes, and has become an excellent negotiator, particular for children's causes, and is an asset to the Nation. Another Libra rising, Winston Churchill, was so inept at school that his teachers despaired of him. Later he worked tirelessly using his diplomatic insightful wisdom against the might of Nazi tyranny during the second World War. Libra energy seems to display it's finest qualities when involved in the cut and thrust with a strong and forceful opponent.

At some stage on the Libra Ascendant journey, it may be necessary to explore both the masculine and feminine sides of life. Usually this Ascendant can struggle with both sides of this dynamic. To give an example, a friend of mine with Sun in Gemini and a Libra Ascendant always struggled with her need to serve both sides of her nature. She achieves this by balancing her working life managing a marketing company in which she needs the sharp cutting edge of the thinking mind to negotiate with many professional men and women, and her personal life as a Mother and supportive partner to the Father of her two children, in which she expresses her softer feeling feminine side. This has always been a challenge for her during her early life as she felt that one excluded the other, but as she matures she is gradually getting those Libra scales in balance. This gift of embracing both sides of their masculine and feminine natures facilitates Libra Ascendant with well rounded negotiating skills in any capacity throughout their lives.

Modern psychology recognises that we are all a mixture of male and female qualities in varying degrees, and that total repression of either leads to some of the worst excesses of human behaviour. Your Libra child needs to recognise their own inner balance between male and female, and many parents could learn something invaluable about their own relationships by experiencing how their child 'marries' their male and female qualities, as it matures.

Ascending signs should always be blended with the relevant Sun and Moon signs in order to find the central motivations of a person. Libra Ascendant will temper any Sun or Moon position to enable the life to become more charming, graceful and harmonious. It is also of note that the planet Saturn is exalted in this sign, indicating that it is through art of right relationship in any sphere that the important lessons are learned in life. And that starts with you, the parent!

FAMOUS LIBRANS
Sun in Libra

Mark Bolan, Brigitte Bardot, Barbara Castle, Edwina Currie, Michael Douglas, Sarah Ferguson, Carrie Fisher, F. Scott Fitzgerald, Alexandra the Great, Bob Geldorf, Charlton Heston, Olivia Newton John, Derek Jacobi, Catherine Zeta Jones, John Lennon, Roger Moore, Ian McShane, Martina Navratilova, George Peppard, Luciano Pavarotti, Christopher Reeve, Cliff Richard, Paul Simon, Michael Stich, Margaret Thatcher, Oscar Wilde.

Moon in Libra

Rory Bremner, Phil Collins, Leonardo Di Caprio, Nicholas Cage, Michael Caine, Walt Disney, John Derek, Grace Kelly, Billy Jean King, Derek Jacobi, Henry Kissenger, Sylvester Stallone.

Libra

Ascendant in Libra

Princess Anne, Leonardo Di Caprio, Winston Churchill, Billy Connolly, Jimmy Connors, Noel Coward, Neil Diamond, Harrison Ford, Cary Grant, Uri Geller, Rock Hudson, George Harrison, J.F. Kennedy, Carole King, Tatum O'Neal, Puccini, Omar Sharif, Cat Stevens, Venus Williams, Denzel Washington.

♏ SCORPIO ♏

Symbolising the Scorpion, the Eagle and the Phoenix representing the three stages of transformation through profound emotional exchange. Scorpio is the second Water Sign.

KEYWORDS: *Intense, secretive, private, passionate, mysterious, dramatic.*

For lust of knowing what should not be known,
we take the Golden Road to Samarkan.

James Elroy Flecker

Scorpio

SUN IN SCORPIO

(Birthday between October 22nd and November 21st)

We must be still, and still moving into another intensity for further union, a deeper communion.

T.S. Eliott

You will only have to look into your Scorpio child's deep and penetrating eyes to realise that you have a powerful little soul in your family. Feel their strong and wiry bodies and quiver at that famous Scorpionic piercing stare and you will instinctively sense that you are going to be in for a very interesting and bumpy ride with this child.

As a fixed water sign you will notice that your child has strong and powerful emotions that are deeply loyal and unchanging. If you make a promise to your Scorpio child, you'd better keep it. They will never, ever forget and definitely will never forgive you if you don't honour your promises. Even at a tender age, a Scorpio child will display great emotional courage and conviction when dealing with others. Fighting for what they believe is just and fair is in-built with these children, and when they fight, they fight! Because of their mystical sixth sense, and X-ray vision, don't mess around with this child's feelings and emotions, they can spot a white lie, psychological game or untruth immediately. Be absolutely straight with this child and you'll be loved and respected for it.

From a very early age, this child seems to know about the deep secrets of life and will sometimes ask some rather embarrassing questions about the mysteries of life and death. Never, never give them a flippant answer or try to avoid their delving questions. Sex is a favourite topic with Scorpio children, who can sniff out embarrassment, taboo and repressed attitudes about the birds and the bees. When they grow up many become psychologists, psychics, healers or indeed anything that gives them an opportunity to exercise their X-ray vision and penetrating insight into the human condition. In fact, anything that takes them into the taboo areas of life which other more simple souls would rather ignore. This child loves challenges and the more difficult and dangerous that challenge is, *the better*. For this reason adolescent Scorpios are often found enjoying the more taboo areas of life without the caution exercised by their peer group. Much of this relates to the key need for Scorpios to achieve self-mastery through crisis and adversity.

Scorpios love to be on the emotional edge of life and will crave the excitement of playing with fire to get the thrills and excitement they so need throughout their lives. Growth by crisis might be their motto. This needs to be recognised by a parent and not suppressed. Your Scorpio child will have very definite ideas of what they want to do and just where they are going. Their power of conviction is awesome and their demanding nature can sometimes be exhausting, but somehow you will admire and respect their ardent convictions. Scorpio firmly believes that to be alive is to be burning which can be pretty hard on a busy mother's time and energies. They need to seek out passion - their's, other's and that of their culture. Try to give them hobbies or physical recreations that allow some of this kind of energy to be released. Life often becomes like a battlefield to your Scorpio child, so try to encourage them to compete in some way, either mentally, physically, emotionally or creatively. Something in Scorpio dies if they do not win or get recognition for what they attempt in life. What you must never do is ignore them, although this is almost an impossibility for they take life and themselves very seriously and persuasively demand attention. Scorpio often wants to know about things that quite frankly, can be a bit uncomfortable to talk about around the dinner table. "How many times do you and mummy have sex?" or "When grandad died, where did he go?" are typical examples. Other signs might wait to ask these questions at bedtime; a Scorpio will often ask them whilst you are entertaining the boss or the vicar.

It would therefore be a good investment to inform your child early on about the birds and the bees, as their blunt and sometimes direct questions could lead to some embarrassing moments, as not everybody will appreciate their need to delve deeply into life. Scorpios see sexual energy as a transformational process; this is because they ardently wish to empower themselves, their partner and eventually the World around them. This child is going to be someone and make a difference in the World, make no mistake about that. Martin Luther King, Richard Burton, Katherine Hepburn and Pablo Picasso all passionately lived out their dynamic and charismatic Scorpionic energy.

Often an intensely private child, Scorpios will need and will in fact demand that you respect their privacy and secrets, but trying to hide things from them is almost impossible. Scorpio children are fearless and have more than their fair share of courage, particularly if they feel unjustly treated. They need you to be firm and fair when dealing with them, but if they sense that you are afraid to define the rules for any reason, you could have a very manipulative child on your hands indeed. These children respect firm and fair discipline and honest explanations. They will pick up immediately on all the things that you would rather not have them know as they seem to have a telephone line to the underworld of your mind. What they do admire is that you share power and trust with them so you can benefit from the exchange of energy which makes the parental bond stronger. One of the greatest lessons you can teach your child is to share - their emotions, fears and dreams. Once your child learns to use and share their power and respect yours, they become truly a servant of their gift of plumbing the depths of life for it's meaning. For if their deep insight into life and to people is abused (ab-*used*), it will surely back-fire on them in some pretty unpleasant ways.

This child will need firm discipline and you will certainly have your work cut out for you in helping them appreciate that not everybody approaches life with their ardour and passion and that some of us like to live relatively simple, peaceful, uncomplicated lives. And tell them when life seems emotionally dangerous that they too need to develop some of this simplicity, developing a sense of inner peace and tranquillity on their journey through life. It need not always be filled

Moon

with crisis. They can learn this lesson well from their opposite sign of Taurus, the Bull.

One good way of understanding the behaviour of this sign is to recognise how important sharing is to your Scorpionic child. They will have to learn that resources are to be shared and renewed. Withholding anything, physical or emotional, sets this sign into immediate action. Many Scorpios consequently work in recycling, environmental control, the money markets and psychotherapy. Relationship problems, either personal or professional, often stem from an inability to share, and many therapists working in the sphere of complex relationships where understanding the art of giving and receiving have this sign strongly emphasised. Give this child all the love and affection their passionate nature craves and you will be rewarded with the love and deep affection of this gifted and special child who right from an early age will have a deep respect for life and all it's challenges. Although you may feel all your preconceived taboos on the deeper aspects of life shaken out from within, it never does any harm to allow a child to show true depth of feeling to its parents. With Scorpio, that's definitely on offer.

Moon in Scorpio

To err is human; to forgive is not our policy.

Anon

When you are in the presence of your Scorpio Moon child, just remember to get your spade out - it's time to do some emotional digging! Right from an early age, your child will display an emotional intensity that will amaze you and even shock you on occasions. You have an emotional warrior in the house. Remember that this is a fixed water sign, so the emotions of this sometimes stubborn enigmatic Moon are sometimes black and white. Scorpio finds it hard to find the middle ground, particularly where their emotions and feelings are concerned. Liz Taylor (Scorpio Moon, Libra Ascendant) epitomises this dilemma in her life and also in one of her best known films *Who's Afraid of Virginia Wolf?* You may find your child will also leave not one stone unturned in their effort to find the emotional truth underlying a situation. Parents must meet this challenge with total integrity for Scorpios suffer fools not at all, let alone gladly!

This sign has great emotional stamina and a taste for intensity and passion. This Moon sign has great depth and likes to probe and risk great honesty in their interaction with others, which can be exhausting for those around them. This kind of self-absorption seems a little out of fashion in this age where intellectual and civilised exchanges are more valued, as someone, even a child, probing the depths of our emotions can frighten people away. This will not bother your Scorpio Moon in the slightest, who will not tolerate the emotionally weak or vulnerable among us. They will energetically demand the attention they need and woe betide you if you do not recognise their need for deep interchange of feeling. When repressed or abused, you might expect some pretty manipulative and covert ways of getting their needs met on this level.

Try to be as honest as you can with your Scorpio and never, ever ignore them, for they take life and themselves very seriously. If you make a promise to your child, keep it. Whilst Scorpio Sun never forgets, Scorpio Moon will never forget, nor stop extracting revenge for any sleight, and forgiveness is out of the question unless you retract and begin being more emotionally honest. This will engender an atmosphere of deep trust between you which this Moon definitely needs. Equal empowerment and trust are BIG issues for this Moon in their emotional exchanges with others, both personally, socially and professionally.

This child will have a temper and if you can co-operate with their need to 'blow off' emotional steam occasionally, this will help them immensely in releasing some of their pent-up emotions which pulse so virulently in their veins. Try to understand that this is a complex sign which seems to have a direct connection to the underworld of your mind, picking up things that you would rather keep to yourself. If you

Moon

come from a family which has a high level of repression in emotional matters, your little Scorpio Moon will plumb the depths to expose it all! Trying to repress your child's feelings or finding such displays of emotion unacceptable could lead to deep emotional damage to your child which will be hard to deal with as they get older. They in turn, need to know that there is a correct time and a right place for such deeply personal things to be discussed.

Finding a place for your child to act out the kaleidoscope of their rich imaginations and emotions is terribly important. Perhaps letting them stage their own play, reading one on their own poems or performing one of their favourite songs. Joni Mitchell, the 'High Priestess of Song' has Sun in Scorpio and if you listen to her songs they display all the deep penetrating insight of the depths of the human soul, which touches her audience deeply. Scorpios hold a fascination for the mysteries of birth, life and death, so be prepared for some demanding and tricky questions from time to time.

Scorpio needs an arena where they can put their hearts and souls into a project which will satisfy and hold their intense emotions for a while. One of the greatest lessons you can teach your Scorpio Moon is to share and trust. Once your child learns to use and share their power with trust, they become truly a servant of their gift of always seeming to know what the other person is feeling and thinking with their X-ray vision and telepathic mind. Endeavour to teach your Scorpio Moon child that not everybody approaches life with their emotional zeal and passion and that some of us like to live relatively simple, peaceful and uncomplicated lives - or we think we do!!

Perhaps eventually they will grow to cultivate some of this simplicity, eventually developing a sense of inner peace and tranquillity which is so important for this sometimes crisis ridden Moon. This child needs your love and affection wholeheartedly. This is a jealous and possessive energy, so constant re-assurance of your loyalty and constancy is important for this sometimes difficult to understand challenging child. Try to give this child all the love and affection their passionate nature craves and you will be rewarded with the love and deep affection of this very special child, who knows how to keep a promise and will never let you down.

Scorpio

ASCENDANT IN SCORPIO

The truth is rarely pure and never simple.

Oscar Wilde

With this Ascendant, life should be approached in an intense and passionate way. Nothing can be taken at face value and often it is very compelling for this Ascendant to search for the underlying meanings and motivations of any issue of life. As such they make good detectives, analysts, psychologists and counsellors. Many are drawn to the healing professions where they can use their great powers of concentration to work with crisis, healing the sick. With their deep understanding and connection to the undertow of life they could be drawn to working with people in crisis or who have been badly let down by family or society. Acting and performing can also be a wonderful outlet for their rich and dramatic emotions, and the regular release of emotions should be encouraged with this Ascendant, otherwise it could result in deep repression for the child resulting in illness and depression. Michael Douglas (Scorpio Ascendant) conveyed his intense style of acting in the film *Fatal Attraction* - a very Scorpionic theme.

Anything that involves the experience of life and death or of being close to the edge will bring this Ascendant to life. To be alive is to be experiencing passion is the motto of this Ascendant, for life itself is often a battleground for Scorpio. These children will approach situations as a warrior prepared for battle, yet are very sensitive to the emotional undercurrents in their environment. Any secrets or withheld

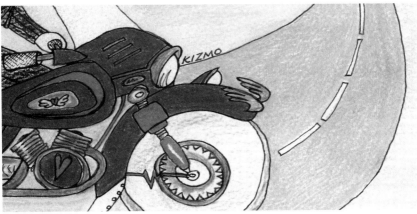

Ascendant

information hidden within the family will be ultimately exposed. Because of this you should work towards an emotionally honest relationship with your child. If you can achieve this emotional balance, you will reap the rewards by seeing your child contribute their powerful ability to understanding life with all it's complexity and helping others to understand this part of their nature. Developing trust in their approach to people and life's situations needs to be developed aiding deep integrity in all their interchanges with others.

Look straight back into those magnetic and piercing eyes, answer with your truth, and your little Scorpio child will honour you and give that ultimate Scorpio gift - their trust and deep respect which enriches and empowers you both in your journey together through life.

FAMOUS SCORPIOS

Sun in Scorpio

Prince Andrew, Prince Charles, Tom Conti, Charles Bronson, Christian Bernard, Benjamin Britten, Richard Burton, John Cleese, Marie Curie, Hilary Clinton, George Elliot, Edward VII, Jodie Foster, Charles De Gaulle, Oliver Goldsmith, Terry Gilliam, Whoopi Goldberg, Billy Graham, Indira Gandhi, Rock Hudson, Goldie Horn, Nigel Havers, Martin Luther King, Billy Jean King, Robert Kennedy, Grace Kelly, Veronica Lake, Lulu, Viscount Linley, Vivian Leigh, Hedy Lamarr, Cleo Laine, Field Marshall Montgomery, Francios Mitterand, Tatum O'Neal, Pablo Picasso, General George Patton, Ezra Pound, Lester Piggott, Gary Player, Sylvia Plath, Erwin Rommel, Jonathan Ross, Helen Reddy, Theodore Roosevelt, Bram Stoker (Dracula), Elke Sommer, Robert Louis Stevenson, Dyland Thomas, Voltaire, Sir Christopher Wren, Auberon Waugh.

Moon in Scorpio

Charles Chaplin, Barbara Cartland, Phil Collins David Frost, Uri Geller, Whoopi Goldberg, Barry Gibb, Lena Horne, Joni Mitchell, Bette Midler, Bob Monkhouse, Steve Martin, Nostradamas, Stephen Spielberg, Liz Taylor.

Scorpio

Ascendant in Scorpio

Casanova, Maria Callas, Charles Chaplin, John Foster Dulles, Michael Douglas, Clint Eastwood, Sigmund Freud, Sarah Ferguson, Aretha Franklin, Geothe, Victor Hugo, Katherine Hepburn, Charlton Heston, Julio Inglesais, Michael Jackson, Grace Kelly, Jacqueline Kennedy, Helen Keller, Mussolini, Edith Piaf, Jack Nicklaus, Patricia Routledge, Rubens, Rudolf Steiner, Claudia Schiffer, Margaret Thatcher, Tracy Ullman, Robin Williams.

SAGITTARIUS

The sign symbolises the Archer, representing the bow and arrow aimed heavenward in search of the higher selfhood. Sagittarius is the 3rd Fire Sign.

KEYWORDS: *Inspirational, lucky, enthusiastic, adventurous, wanderer or quester, philosophical.*

Everybody loves the sound of the train in the distance.
Paul Simon

Sagittarius

SUN IN SAGITTARIUS

(Birthday between November 22nd and December 21st)

Right from the word 'go' you will notice that your Sagittarius child will have a hunger for life and all it's experiences. Indeed, the word 'go' holds great meaning for Sagittarians. They will throw themselves into whatever takes their fancy with enthusiasm and abandon. Jupiter, the planet ruling this sign, is the largest planet in the solar system, thus Sagittarians aspire to become the biggest, grandest and the best. Jupiter conveys a certain charm and good fortune onto these souls who, often unfortunately, think they are always entitled to it. Your child will have such a winning way and will appear to be born with a lucky streak.

In myth Jupiter was the King of the Gods and you will see this trait in your little Sagittarian - who expects immediate attention, and often a fan-fare and a drum roll when they enter the room. And the strange thing is, you won't be able to refuse them this attention either, for their enthusiasm is highly infectious and the Sagittarian warmth so appealing as to be irresistible. In smallish doses, that is, for too much Sagittarius can be exhausting for everyone. Sagittarians always seem to know where the social action is - the best party, that wonderful new restaurant that's just opened where all the glamorous people congregate, for they love to soak up the vibrations of those people in high places. The late socialite Paula Yates was a wonderful example of this energy with her Sagittarian Ascendant.

Something inside a Sagittarius knows that they are special and that they deserve the best that life can give. This optimistic, happy-go-lucky approach to life often does bestow your Sagittarius with great luck and bounty, and seems to attract people and experiences which enable them to accomplish their dreams, which can be very big, even 'mega' or over-the-top. Sagittarians have a freedom-loving and adventurous spirit and are keen to take any challenge that life presents them. They truly believe that they are blessed and that life will provide.

'Don't fence me in' might be their slogan and woe betide anybody who tries to keep your little Sagittarius under lock and key. They find

Sun

it hard to tolerate any form of restriction or boundary. They can't stand limitations, for their eyes are always drawn to the distant broad horizon where life beckons to be better than it is in the here and now of reality. Try not to crush or ridicule their dreams, but at the same time, for their own protection, let them know that it will be necessary for them to define and cope with reasonable limitations occasionally.

Sagittarius are the seekers and questers of life and they are always trying to find the answers to the 'meaning of life'. They ask, 'What is the meaning of my life - why am I here?' Their quest to find the answers to these kinds of philosophical questions can lead them up many paths and over many distant horizons. Even if you have one of the more reserved or cautious Sagittarians they will still travel in their minds and imaginations to far away places. Life is always beckoning them over the next horizon, whether they are introverted or extroverted. The truth or the quest is always in the distance. With this in mind, it is as well to provide them with a good education, one that could lead on to expanding their knowledge enabling them to promote, teach or lecture about their chosen subject at a later stage in life. They need an educational process where they learn two essentials, a focus or 'narrowing down' the field of view or the vision to a manageable level, and then to finish what they start. Sagittarius is a notorious sign for taking up fads and sudden obsessive interests which start well but peter out as the next project overtakes everything.

Sagittarius

Life's a journey for Sagittarius - arriving is not the main goal. Indeed, the journey ends at arrival so let's keep on travelling is their motto. Steven Spielberg's (Sun in Sagittarius) film *The Raiders of the Lost Ark* is a typical Sagittarian journey, concerned with a quest and finding the treasure. Sagittarius is also the gypsy of the Zodiac and is

far more excited by the travelling and what they find whilst they are travelling, than the actual arrival. Whoever said "it is better to travel than to arrive" must have been a Sagittarian. Don't be surprised if you hear your little Sagittarius asking questions about faraway places, and telling you of their dreams to visit those places one day. For whether you child travels inwardly, in their imaginations,or outwardly in the World, rest assured their mind and heart are always attracted to those far horizons where they can experience different cultures and rituals and compare them with their own.

Like Christopher Columbus (Sun in Sagittarius), Sagittarians are explorers and always on the look out for those lucky encounters that bring new and exciting challenges. There's something of a gambler in Sagittarius, and certainly this sign is associated with risk taking. You might find your explorative little Archer promising to travel one day. Always encourage them to have something to look forward to, a goal or intention, as this is so important for them and their emotional well being. If this is not possible, try to get them books and videos that appeal to their sense of adventure and travel. They may talk about settling in a foreign country one day, as they will become so interested in foreign people and different cultures. Sagittarius is the long distance traveller whilst their opposite sign, Gemini, likes to travel over short distances, usually within their local environment.

With their eyes always on the horizon, it is important to encourage your child to look in the rear view mirror from time to time, attending to the everyday aspects of life and realising some of their dreams of exploring the meaning of life. For like their symbol, the Archer with his

Sun

bow and arrow, they need firm ground in order to aim straight and true so that their dreams are not to be lost in the sky. Because they have a great appetite for life and all it's pleasures, it is as well to keep an eye on their diet, for like the expansive planet Jupiter, their ruler, if their appetite for life is not being satisfied, they could over-eat and drink to make up for this lack. Henry the Eighth was a magnificent example of Sagittarian energy with his generous and gifted nature. As a young man his popularity and lust for life (he was the first ever tennis star), earned him the nickname 'Good King Hal'; his later appetite for food and women eventually became excessive, leading to his own physical undoing.

Sagittarius is the showman of the Zodiac and many are drawn to the theatre or into promotional activities. Sagittarius is a true promoter and salesperson. They seem to have a deep connection to what is going to be popular and what will appeal to the public. Many political leaders such as Ronald Reagan (Sagittarius Ascendant) and Winston Churchill (Sun in Sagittarius) have the ability to inspire people with their enthusiasm and belief that, in times of trouble and depression, everything will turn out all right in the end.

No sign makes you laugh like a Sagittarian, witness Billy Connolly and Woody Allen, and no sign can help you believe in yourself again after a fall or disappointment Their enthusiasm and generosity of spirit is very infectious, and nothing shocks them. Against this, Sagittarians are blunt, frank and often highly unsubtle. This is the 'in-your-face' sign, often spurred into outbursts of temper which flare up quickly with the intensity of a tropical hurricane only to die away equally quickly leaving not a trace of malice. Sagittarians say what they mean and their language is often highly colourful which may burst out at inappropriate times and places. Mozart's Moon position, and Beethoven's Sun and Moon were in Sagittarius, and the behaviour and language of this pair of musical geniuses was legendary. If any other sign behaved in this way, there would be outrage, yet often the Sagittarian somehow gets away with it, and their charm and glitter remains intact, if a little tarnished.

Sagittarius

The French word *sagesse* means wisdom, from which our word 'sage' is derived. But this is not necessarily the wisdom of the mind, but a deeply connected intelligence which intuitively knows and believes that everything in this world is linked and therefore worth learning about. If you have the more studious type of Sagittarius it is wise to encourage them to develop their expansive thought systems through religious or philosophical studies. The sign does have a propensity for evangelising, soap-box oratory, lecturing and preaching and this can be a terrible bore if some subtlety and wisdom has not been learned. When the true wisdom of this sign shines through, your child will eventually be able and ready to serve society with the fire of his/her intelligence and courageous visions.

MOON IN SAGITTARIUS

Man is great in his intentions, but weak in carrying the out. Therein lies our misery and our charm.

Charles Boyer

The needs of your Sagittarius Moon child are huge. This is a very hungry moon indeed, associated with restlessness which means hungry for all the bounty that life can offer, the restlessness coming through attempting to 'have it all'. The sheer lust for life of this Moon position is remarkable and may mean that your Sagittarius Moon child will need nothing less than everything. Your child will need to make a big statement about their life. Observe their speech and mannerisms and you will notice that this child loves to exaggerate their experiences. In their imagination life should be led and experienced in the shortest period of time, which may result in a lack of concentration and a certain defocussing.

Never crush their dreams or their gushes of dramatic outpouring as these are very important to their well-being, for they consider them not to be a waste of time. They intend to make some of their dreams come true and given the right love and support, they will. As their parent, you may find a child with this Moon position exceptionally demanding, and at times exhausting with their unquenchable lust for life. With their friendly and optimistic natures, these children are natural gamblers with time, money, other people and life. This child's

Moon

enthusiasm and imagination is boundless and "anything is possible" as well as "safety last" might well be their ideal mottoes. Unlike the Earth signs, who build something up slowly during their lives and reap the rewards in old age, such a life-plan doesn't appeal to Sagittarians at all. Boring! They love the idea that life is perhaps like betting on a horse, with the thrill of not knowing what the outcome will be, while believing that they will win and will return home victorious.

Freedom is their watchword and "Don't fence me in" the cry of this adventurous Moon. Woe betide you if you try to restrict their desperate need for space, either physically or emotionally. They just love the outdoors and those wide open spaces. You will find that they are probably attracted to horses, an animal which symbolises the instinctual side of the sign - and also the freedom of spirit with which this sign is identified. Perhaps they might like to take up riding as a recreation to get them in touch with this side of their nature. Many sports personalities, racing drivers and motorcyclists have this sign strongly placed in their astrological charts. A parent must balance the risks carefully against the potential learning advantages in their child's need for adventure. Timid parents who err on the cautious side will probably encourage the risk taking as the child rebels against what it sees as boring and mundane behaviour imposed by a restrictive authority figure. Over authoritarian parenting similarly should be avoided: remember Mozart's difficult relationship with his oppressive father. Try to remember what it was like to be young and free once again, and you're half-way to understanding a Sagittarian child.

These tendencies can result in what seems like a lack of commitment in any walk of life, but what your Sagittarius Moon is committed to is *The Quest*, their journey and finding the meaning of their life and how they can live life to the full and become enriched by their experiences. This is their nourishment - not a pipe and slippers by the fireside. Their questing nature leads them up some pretty interesting and sometimes hazardous avenues, but whether your child travels in their inner life or literally in the physical world, you must let them. They will return, like the Prodigal Son bearing the gift of wisdom learnt from their expansive, risky and near-to-the-edge experiences.

Because of their untamed and adventurous spirit, you might find it a challenge to discipline your child and you might here the cry "Don't tell me what to do!!" The secret is to ASK your child nicely and try to give them a reason why they should do something and hopefully you'll get a positive reaction. You'll hear the word WHY? a lot coming from Sagittarians as they will want to know everything and won't be content with a superficial answer, so always have your mind ready for their enthusiastic and expansive questions. Although difficult, encourage them to look after their money and take care of their body. The body can be a real nuisance to Sagittarius as it needs rest, food and sleep and Sagittarius often does not have much time for this. If anyone was to invent a candle that had three ends to burn, Sagittarius would buy it. There's always that next adventure, party or creative scheme beckoning.

Fire signs are often very impatient with the practical side of life, and unless your Sagittarius Moon has some earth in their chart they may avoid like the plague the mundane, dreary, day-to-day reality and routine. The acquisition of money for the fire signs is often a means to an end and is not really part of their reality. Be prepared some-times to face the famous Sagittarius temper tantrum, which can be quite dramatic and theatrical. This usually arises because they feel frustrated by the limitations that life inevitably imposes on them or perhaps they have become bored and want to stir things up a little. Boredom is the big enemy of this Moon position, and may result in periods of depression.

Sagittarius does everything in BIG way and feels frustrated with anything that they consider mediocre. Sometimes there is more than a touch of arrogance with this Moon. So get your child to join the local drama group, the hiking club, outward bound or flying school - anything that appeals to that adventurous spirit. Keep their exploratory and questing nature alive by rekindling it whenever enthusiasm wanes. Invest in a good education for your child - this Moon position can become very tedious if undernourished with the lack of a good education.

Ascendant

ASCENDANT IN SAGITTARIUS

And the trouble is if you don't risk anything, you risk even more.
Erica Jong - *Fear of Flying*

With this Ascendant, life should be approached in an optimistic and independent way. Life should be viewed as a journey or pilgrimage which will result in your child finding answers to the many questions that will be asked during their lives. Improving the mind through travel, education and exploration will help your child satisfy their hunger for knowledge and information. Sagittarians have the ability to inspire others with their generosity of spirit and enthusiasm for life and make good leaders, teachers and philosophers. But if this energy is dissipated through idle dreaming within the unfathomable realm of possibilities, then the energy and gift of this Ascendant may become wasted. Sometimes there is a tendency for extravagance and overdoing life if they 'steer too close to the wind' which can result in excess and wastefulness, which can also affect your child's health and well being. It is best to encourage your child to work towards grounding or finding a realistic channel for their aspirations through the route of teaching, acting, travelling, publishing, selling or promoting their visionary ideals.

With this Ascending sign, the rules, boundaries and natural limitations of life need to be learned, understood and integrated into all walks of their life. As for all fiery Ascendants, it is important to get enough rest and to take care of the body through developing some form

Sagittarius

of disciplined recreational sports activity such as horse riding, archery, motor-cycling, hiking, rock climbing, dancing or body work. It's a busy life being a Sagittarian Ascendant, so much to do and so little time to do it all!

FAMOUS SAGITTARIANS

Sun in Sagittarius

Jane Austen, Woody Allen, Beethoven, Busby Berkeley, William Blake, Hector Berlioz, Kim Basinger, Dave Brubeck, Ian Botham, Noel Coward, Jimmy Connolly, Joseph Conrad, Winston Churchill, Maria Callas, David Carradine, Andrew Carnegie, Kirk Douglas, Benjamin Disraeli, Walk Disney, Christopher Fry, Jane Fonda, Manuel de Falla, Douglas Fairbanks, Betty Grable, Uri Geller, Paul Getty, Robin and Maurice Gibb (*Spirits having Flown*), Jimi Hendrix, J.F. Kennedy Jr., Henri Toulouse-Loutrec, Jim Morrison, Nancy Mitford, Margaret Mead, Bette Midler, Michael Owen, Christina Onassis, Edith Piaf, Puccini, Carlo Ponti, Bhagwan Shri Rajneesh, Rainer Maria Rilke, Tommy Steele, Frank Sinatra, Steven Spielberg, James Thurber, Mark Twain, Tina Turner, Dionne Warwick.

Moon in Sagittarius

Neil Armstrong, Brahms, Kevin Costner, Copernicus, Albert Einstein, Ian Fleming, Billy Graham, Judy Garland, Bob Geldorf, Rock Hudson, Glenda Jackson, Nichole Kidmann, Carole King, Liszt, Henri Matisse, George Melly, Rupert Murdock, Yoko Ono, Al Pacino, Christopher Reeve (*Superman*), Oprah Winfrey.

Ascendant in Sagittarius

Marlon Brando, Bob Dylan, Princess Diana, Prince William, Marc Bolan, Brigitte Bardot, Nicholas Cage, Bob Geldorf, Jodie Foster, Goldie Hawn, Eartha Kitt, Elvis Presley, Shirley Temple, Alan Shearer, Sylvesta Stallone, Paula Yates.

CAPRICORN

The Sign symbolises the Goat climbing the mountain towards the heights, solitary and alone. Capricorn is the third Earth Sign.

KEYWORDS: *Ambitious, reliable, disciplined, professional, supportive.*

What on earth would we do with ourselves, if something did not stand in our way.

H.G. Wells

Capricorn

SUN IN CAPRICORN
(Birthday between December 22nd and January 21st)

When you look at your tiny Capricorn child, you will get the feeling that you are looking into the eyes of a very wise old soul - someone who's been around for a very long time. Perhaps you may be reminded of Father Christmas, whose sign, Capricorn, is the sign of the benevolent Father - (but only if you've been a *good* child!) - and of maturity and old age. Male or a female, your little 'goat' will display the characteristics of someone who has an old head on their shoulders and who naturally understand the boundaries and limitations that life always imposes. These children will strive to become their own authority at an early stage of their journey through life, and will want to ground their experiences in the world with a pragmatic sense of realism.

Right from the beginning Capricorn seems to be in touch with this principal of independence and of doing things on their own. Capricorn respects autonomy and has a deep connection with the principal of self-sufficiency. Capricorn is the 'rock' of the Zodiac - upon which others may depend. More like the tortoise than the hare in the famous fable, Capricornians know only too well the wisdom of taking their time and working consistently at the 'coal-face' of life, not burning out in a flash of brilliance like the Fire signs sometimes do. Capricornian energy is about the establishment of *self* in the world. A clue to the nature of this sign comes from the word *'establishment'*. Heavy and burdensome, with slow response to change and heavy focus on administration, it defines stable boundaries of behaviour and social structure from which we all ultimately benefit. The greatest shame facing a Capricorn is public disgrace and then rejection for misusing the laws of the land. Fortunately, insistence on staying within the law and adopting ethical behaviour usually earmarks this sign.

Capricorn's ability to conserve and manage energy with stamina enables them to endure, to win the race and climb the mountain by arduous effort, and those born under this sign know that only fools and aspiring pop-stars believe that life is easy and effortless. Craggy ol'

Sun

Capricorn believes in traditional hard work with no short cuts, understanding that in life there are no free lunches nor free loaders and that everything must be paid for in solid coin. Capricorn doesn't trust life if they get things too easy, and firmly believes in sustained effort and in the traditional concept of commitment. Capricorn is a very conservative sign with a deep respect for natural law and history and those born with this Sign strongly marked in their chart will often delight in researching or finding out about the family tree and will tell you all about its members.

Sometimes there could be some difficulty or mystery about the parent's background or there could be an absent parent. Capricorns often have a problem finding a role model for 'father' - seeking it from teachers, priests, authority figures or even God, in addition to their natural father. Often if Capricorn's ruling planet, Saturn, is strong in their chart, it can indicate that the father, or that which father represents to them, will be very important to their early development. Either way, the figure of 'Father' usually looms large throughout a Capricorn's life. Because of this, they normally have a strong attachment to the past, their roots and their ancestors, like their opposite sign of Cancer, the sign of the Mother. Because of their love of continuity, your little Capricorn will be very dutiful and responsible towards their family. You can see this quality in Dolly Parton (Sun in Capricorn) who emotionally and materially supports her whole family following her long climb to success as a Country Singer.

Capricorns love the idea of ritual, rights of passage and all the routine that goes with doing things in a time-honoured way. You will find your child very supportive around the house and they will respect the laws, ceremonies and rituals of family life. Sometimes this structuring becomes burdensome, and gets in the way of spontaneity. This is a very private, shy, and retiring sign and unless they have a good dose of fire in their birth charts, Capricorns will not overtly display their feelings nor seek the limelight. A good example of this behaviour is to be found in Anthony Hopkins, an extremely successful actor, yet who always displays an innate shyness, reserve and humility when being interviewed.

Capricorn is a self-deprecating sign - aware that each of us is but a small cog facilitating the smooth running of the larger human machine - our society and culture. Nevertheless, little goats are ambitious and

Capricorn

will seek to be the best at all they attempt in life. Some of the most ambitious souls you will ever meet come under this sign - it's the manner of achievement which is different. They want to climb, albeit slowly and thoroughly, to the top of their class and be the best at whatever they endeavour to do in life.

Like the other Earth signs of Taurus and Virgo, Capricorns deeply respect and admire the qualities of apprenticeship, craftsmanship and of mastering skills. Many Capricorns (Sun, Moon or Ascendant position) have such a developed gift for shape and form that they become architects, artists, sculptors (Rodin, Sun in Capricorn), engineers, landscape gardeners and designers. But whether they become a road sweeper or chairperson of the board of directors, Capricorn desires and has the grace and sense to work slowly towards being at the 'top of the tree', and then maintaining that position well into old age. This can sometimes make them unpopular, as Capricorn is also the sign of the ulterior motive. They understand the value and skill of not unleashing their power too quickly, thereby losing the desired 'deal' they wish to negotiate.

Innately aware of the social pecking order, this sign more than any other seeks to climb, albeit gracefully, up the ladder of success and achievement.

Talented at closing any desired deal they wish to negotiate, Capricorns understand very early on that life needs to be tamed and harnessed, particularly in understanding and controlling their own and other's instinctual and competitive natures. Those born under this sign are always willing to negotiate, or 'strike a deal' with others in order to attain the success they yearn for so much. They seem to have a sixth sense as to other people's real motivations and are not overly endowed with trust, particularly if to trust means being out of

Sun

control. Ultimately, as a parent, you will have to earn the trust and deep respect of your child. You may find it difficult to get them to show their emotions and it might be as well to re-assure them and make them feel as safe as possible when they are emotionally needy. Capricorns, despite being self-sufficient by nature, have a positive horror of being rejected - from parents, from society or from the job. Like failure, the fear of rejection haunts them. Yet, paradoxically, underneath all that reserve and control lives a very earnest little soul who yearns to be out of control occasionally and to display their powerful emotions. From an early age they may recognise that this might not be welcome and indeed may be unacceptable in the social environment in which they live. A parent should help them live out this more spontaneous side from time to time, teaching and encouraging such activity.

It takes time to develop an intimate relationship with this sign, but if you have the patience, which Capricorn certainly does, then you will have a friend for life in your little child, who will always be caring, loyal and responsible towards you. They will never let you down once you have shown your colours as a reliable and trustworthy parent. As your child gets older, a deep warmth of mutual respect will develop. This is the sign of the mountain goat, remember, and it takes time to climb to the top of whichever 'mountain' is chosen. In fact the word 'time' is very important to a Capricorn, as the sign's ruling planet, Saturn, is also known as Chronos. In Greek myth Chronos ruled time, from which our word chronological derives.

Capricorn cannot bear to be unrecognised or unsuccessful at anything and will sometimes not attempt something at which they cannot excel or where there's a risk of failure. This characteristic can be a real hindrance to your child's development, so try to encourage them be content with what they have achieved so far, and to sometimes try new things which are risky, which may not come right at first. Agree with your child that it takes endurance and patience to overcome obstacles when climbing that mountain of success, but that the odd failure offers knowledge and wisdom about where not to step again!

Your child might show a decided preference for being in the company of their elders and you might find them listening with great interest to grown-up conversations. They seldom have a lot of casual friends, unless they have a lot of air in their chart, and prefer instead to befriend a few trusted souls. Most probably they'll have one special friend with whom they share their trust and personal secrets. This can be a very private child who learns about control and discipline from a very early age and could be sometimes overly concerned with doing the 'right' thing and their 'duty'. The old saying of "work first, play later" applies to this faithful and serious Earth sign, which, frankly, can become very dull if this becomes imbalanced, so that there is no place left for fun and play. "All work and no play makes Jack (Capricorn) a dull boy". And Jill too, of course!

Luckily, you will usually find that when Capricorns feel that they have achieved a goal or done their duty, in whatever capacity, then they have the ability to release the playful side of their nature, as represented by the goat-god Pan, the god of nature and the wild natural places. Then, they can really let their hair down and temporarily suspend that controlled, sometimes introvert side of their nature. The biggest party time of the year used to be Saturnalia, held when the Sun passed into the sign of Capricorn at the Winter Solstice. Capricorn artists like David Bowie, Shirley Bassey and Annie Lennox, who have endured the test of time in a very demanding and difficult business, display this deeply passionate, sensual and creative side of the sign, yet remain professionals to their very finger tips. They understand that when their work is done then they can relax, and no-one can enjoy themselves more than a succesful Capricorn.

MOON IN CAPRICORN

Winter is a great teacher

Sydney Poitier

More than anything else your Moon in Capricorn child will need support and security - lots of it! All children need these things, of course, but with this Moon, your child will need to feel that it stands within a safe structure. The quote from Sydney Poitier relates to his hard and difficult childhood before he became famous as a film actor. The Moon in the horoscope is how we get fed and with this Moon position your child will find nourishment only within a safe and structured family environment. This is a complex and powerful Moon position for it links to Saturn, the ruler of this sign. Saturn is responsible for the setting of limits and constraints and is always

Moon

realistic in the use of energy. Sometimes with this Moon position, the link with Saturn can make the child feel isolated and alone because, as an example, the parents may be engaged pursuing a profession or other duty, either by being at work or by being busy elsewhere within the family. Such situations, however necessary, may land heavily on the child's emotional core and restrict their future expectations in emotional transactions.

Sometimes, at a tender age, a child with this Moon position will be expected to shoulder domestic responsibilities - perhaps by looking after brothers and sisters. This Moon position instinctively understands the life of their busy parents, yet still feels neglected if their needs are not regularly met because the parents are 'too busy' or load extra responsibilities onto their child. Sometimes your child will feel that they have to grow up very quickly because of circumstances that surround them, so do try to make time for this sensitive, shy and deeply conservative little child who may be too timid to ask for your time, a cuddle or a special hug.

You will notice that from an early age your child will display a character of discipline and control and will never expect to get anything easily. In fact they will mistrust any situation where things seem to fall effortlessly into their lap. This can develop into emotional repression, over-cautious behaviour and just plain unhappiness if unchecked. Although they seem programmed to develop emotional self-sufficiency, this does not have to mean emotional withdrawal from life. Because they sense that it is a tough place out there in the World they do need to build up their defence mechanisms in order to protect themselves from the blows of life which they innately expect will come their way. This can lead to a determined and self-protective outlook on life, which is an admirable quality in their future professional lives, but not at all helpful in their emotional one. So, try to encourage your serious Moon Capricorn child to enjoy life just for the sheer fun of it. Tell the child that not everything they attempt in life has to have a goal or even a purpose. Get them to wear a silly hat and blow a few raspberries occasionally!

Capricorn

Naturally tenacious, when this Moon position commences a task, it is pursued until the goal is realised. Capricorns never give up and they pursue their goals with great clarity and focus. Starting something can be difficult for them because of their strong streak of perfectionism and self criticism can sometimes paralyse their progress. The symbol of Capricorn is actually a goat with a fish's tail and this suggests that your goat can also swim in the waters of their emotional life, which they should be encouraged to do. Sometimes, as a parent, you may need to remind your goat-child that it can get pretty lonely up at the craggy peak of their own personal 'mountain'. Perhaps too you might encourage your Moon Capricorn by reminding them that we get the word *cornucopia*, or 'horn of plenty', from the abundance of the Earth. Encourage them to climb their  particular 'mountain' slowly, step by step. Taking their time, they will achieve their goals and find their abundance, something which is so important to them. Whilst young, this child needs recognition and support from you, and eventually from the World, and will naturally follow a route towards some kind of professional status.

If money is not easy to come by within the family, your Capricorn Moon will understand that money and developing a sense of independence through the acquisition of resources will enable them to enjoy the kind of life which augments their naturally independent nature. In excess this can become meanness and Scrooge like - A 'Christmas Carol' is a very Capricornian story! The thought of being dependent on anyone or anything is horrendous to this strongly self-reliant Moon. We can see this quality in the artist Cher, who has dedicated herself to her career as a singer and actress with all the tenacity and dedication of her Capricorn Moon. True to the longevity of this sign, she maintains her position at the top of her profession after a long and competitive career.

Ascendant

This is not a stay at home Moon, although it is very sensitive to the family and all it's traditions and to its duty within the family. The gift of this Moon is in it's capacity to nurture by providing for its loved ones in a realistic, tangible and professional way, thereby teaching others the wisdom and beauty of contributing to life with the knowledge that one is completely self-reliant. Encouragement to develop this quality will pay dividends for a parent who experiences the early autonomy of their Capricorn Moon-child.

ASCENDANT IN CAPRICORN

You achieve more if you know your limitations.

Aesop's Fables

With this Ascendant life needs to be approached in a practical and persistent way with the accent on achieving and attaining goals and objectives. The drive for success and recognition is often exceedingly strong in whatever field your child pursues. This is the sign of the professional performer and Capricorn rising needs to work slowly towards their goal of achieving professional status at some time in their lives. Energy should be carefully measured out, a practice which calls for discipline and control.

Capricorn rules the knees in the physical body, this symbolises that the higher we climb in life, the more humility and grace we need to develop, eventually bending to limitations and frustrations that are met with whilst climbing to the top of their chosen profession. In prayer we kneel in submission to a higher authority than ourselves. Your child needs to be encouraged to methodically make something of themselves so that they can eventually command the respect and validation they seek from the world and their peers. In the process they should not loose respect for higher authorities.

Patience should be cultivated, for like good wine, Capricorn matures slowly, but matures well. This sign is usually blessed with a long life, giving them the time needed to see the fruits of their hard-won labours reach maturity. Establishment within the order of things matters a great deal to this Ascendant. Often they arrive into this world with burdensome conditions and limitations, so that they get their lessons in caution, reticence and thrift extremely early on, because there is a sense of lack of support which may never be forthcoming. With this Ascendant, they are taught the need for a realistic outlook right from the start of life. The benefits from this lesson are that less time is wasted in frivolous amusement. There is a shrewd quality of reserve and watchfulness which marks out children with this sign rising. They often have a gift for knowing the inner motivations of those they meet, and the motives of those with whom they work. This gift is forged from struggling with their own inner issues of learning to trust in life's bounty. Perhaps as a parent, you would be best advised to guide your child into recognising that this bounty is truly all around them, and that their task is to become skilled at harvesting it. Then *cornucopia*, the 'goat-horn of plenty' becomes truly their birth-right.

FAMOUS CAPRICORNIANS

Sun in Capricorn

Michael Aspel, Joan Baez, David Bowie, David Bellamy, Shirley Bassey, Paul Cezanne, Kevin Costner, Marlene Dietrich, Faye Dunaway, Gerard Depardieu, John Denver, Benjamin Franklin, Mel Gibson, Ava Gardner, Stephen Hawking, Henry Miller, Anthony Hopkins, Janis Joplin, Diana Keaton, Johannes Kepler, Rudyard Kipling, Annie Lennox, Tom Keating, Henri Matisse, Isaac Newton, Richard Nixon, Aristotle Onassis, Elvis Presley, Dolly Parton, Rodin, Albert Schweitzer, Jon Voight.

Moon in Capricorn

Clara Barton, Cher, Neil Diamond, Michael Douglas, Federico Fellini, Billy Holiday, Ernest Hemmingway, Annie Lennox, Yehudi Menuhin, Dean Martin, Carl Rogers, Robert Redford, Donna Summer, Alan Shearer, Stephen Sondheim, Tammy Wynette, George Washington.

Ascendant in Capricorn

Queen Elizabeth II, Sean Connery, Barbara Castle, Jane Fonda, Dustin Hoffman, Buddy Holly, Anthony Hopkins, Billy Jean King, Sophia Loren, Liberace, Yehudi Menuhin, Michaelangelo, Paul Newman, Leonardo da Vinci.

AQUARIUS

The sign symbolises the Water Carrier/Bearer pouring the waters of life onto humanity and is the 3rd Air Sign.

KEYWORDS: *Inventive, progressive, unpredictable, eccentric, humanitarian, controlled emotions.*

There are no perfect people in this World, only perfect intentions.

Anon

SUN IN AQUARIUS

(Birthday between January 21st and February 21st)

If you have a child born with the Sun in Aquarius you will wonder at times whether they have arrived from another planet. Astrologers place this sign under the rulership of that strange and revolutionary planet Uranus, since that planet's discovery in 1781, prior to the French, American and Industrial Revolutions. So expect the unexpected and be prepared for some pretty unpredictable behaviour and don't count on your child conforming to any kind of daily routine. You truly have a free spirit in your midst, someone who is inclined to break the rules and who will stubbornly resist any routine which fails to suit their view of matters. And what are those matters? Well, Aquarians are not particularly happy on the Earth plane unless they are trying to change things down here. They want to understand and then improve the human condition - artistically, socially, politically and environmentally. Because of this, individuals are not always seen as terribly important, whilst organisations, groups and communities assume a greater importance. Aquarians are primarily wanting to change the future and thus they often feel like an outsider - a stranger in a strange land. And many of them behave like Spock from Star Trek, though without the silly ears of course!

Aquarius is a fixed sign, yet much of the above paragraph leads us to expect tumultuous changes. To explain this apparent paradox, one must understand the traditional co-rulership of this sign by the planet Saturn. Underpinning every brilliant Aquarian vision or new idea, is the grounding effect of Saturn which is, thankfully, never far behind to set it within the realms of reality. Their gift is to take 'the known' and build it into something unknown. This modifies the positive fixity of the sign, as it endows them with the ability to be realistic within group situations and collective endeavours. Your Aquarian child will have a strong sense of their own individuality and will want to do things their way, or not at all, yet will eventually, be able to see the collective way to solve human and social problems.

Sun

Aquarian children can be as stubborn as can all the fixed signs, but as an air sign, are often much quicker and cleverer with their intellect. They can often twist and argue their way out of any argument, claiming that logical thought wins the day. Fitting in with those around them or attending to those boring everyday routines like cleaning teeth or even feeding themselves adequately presents many Aquarians with their toughest tests in life. Instead, your little space cadet would rather watch sci-fi films and read about dinosaurs, spaceflight or the outer fringes of science and high-tech, identifying with all those concepts that transport them to another planet or dimension of life.

They will display a keen interest in new and futuristic technology and techniques which appeal to their sense of improving the lot of

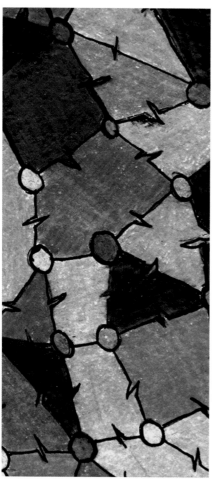

mankind. As your child gets older, you may like to tell them about the myth of Prometheus, who stole fire from Zeus, the King of the Olympian Gods, and then gave it back to humanity. In the myth he was punished by Zeus for his act of service. Sometimes this theme appears in the life of Aquarians if they step over and beyond their human limitations in any way, or ignore their own bodily needs. Both the human body and the cosmos guard their secrets well and for good reason. The body is a temple, a microcosm of the Universe, but it is an unrealistic task to explain this to a difficult three-year old who won't put his raincoat on or eat his meals, because there is something much more exciting to discover!

Aquarians are the true anarchists and reformers of our world. The Aquarian dream - that each one of us should have equal

Aquarius

opportunities and equal rights requires that we be really evolved as human beings. Your child may need to have explained to them, when a little older, that this cannot happen unless they fully engage with and understand the processes of human life. What you can help them understand is that sometimes it is necessary to accept limitations and boundaries, as there will always be something or someone out there in the world who will refute their prophetic visions, and oppose their dreams. This brings about the blessing or successful blending of their co-ruler, Saturn, without which all their ideals may come to little other than conceptual castles in the air.

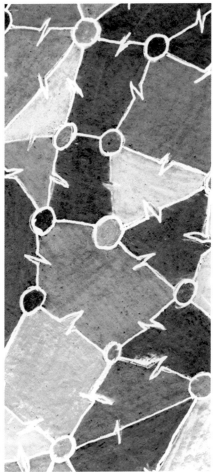

Aquarians are often way ahead of their time, and appear awkward, ill-adapted or just plain eccentric as a consequence. The sign's new ruler, Uranus is a huge clue as to your child's true nature. Don't therefore be surprised if you have a few problems with teachers at school who find it hard to understand that your child has arrived at an answer to their questions before they've even had time to finish writing it on the blackboard! They might even consider school to be a boring waste of time. This child is a human computer and it would wise to consider some form of unstructured education for them such as Montessori or Steiner/Waldorf where they are contained, but are allowed to be more free or more radical in their expression. Don't be surprised too if they display traits of absent-mindedness, never remembering where they left anything or what you last asked them to do. This child's mind is far beyond such mundane trivia and likes to disappear into the wonderful world of thought and concept. Their heads

Sun

can often be like Dr Who's Tardis - a multi-dimensional passport to strange new worlds. Dr Who is an archetypal Aquarian concept, and the very first episode of this most popular children's sci-fi programme was even entitled 'A Strange Child'.

But there are stunning rewards to be enjoyed from your eccentric, sometimes detached little one. Once you can understand that you are responsible for a non-conformist who needs to be allowed to develop in their own way, life can become immediately easier and more interesting for both parents and child. Aquarians often have minds sharper than razor blades and you will notice a touch of the 'mad professor' about them, with periodic flashes of genius. They can often come up with the solution to a question by the strangest routes - inbuilt lateral thinking is one of their greatest gifts.

Try to be patient with your child if they show no interest at all in the more practical things like eating and getting dressed, for they definitely have their own rhythms, own style and are never slaves to the latest fashion, yet often define its future path. They will often forget their knickers, or wear the clothes of the opposite sex, wear odd socks or clash colours. Your Uranian child naturally loves to shock, even in some seemingly inconsequential ways, and many Aquarians cross the barriers of gender, race or sexuality without a second thought. "Liberation" is their banner, along with "fraternity" and "equality" - just remember the French Revolution slogan to know your child.

Aquarians are known as the humanitarians of society. As potential pioneers and visionaries of society's future they usually take a keen

interest in their fellow man and the plight of civilisation and environment, even at an early age. As the collective air sign, it is a most exciting concept for them to share a common bond with their friends. So be prepared for lots of parties and meetings where your child can be with their sometimes eccentric friends. Just remind yourself, amongst all the chaos and spilt jelly, that your little 'space cadet' is going to make a difference to society. Aquarius is known as the architect of the Zodiac, and dreams of serving mankind with their unusual and often 'light-years ahead' brilliant ideas. And what parent would want to switch off such an illuminating vision?

They are loyal to their friends and love to make contact with other people, whilst retaining their sense of freedom and independence. If they are going to make a difference to society, they intuitively know that they need to remain detached from the emotionally complex part of human relationships - the messy bits - which could distract them from their goals. Aquarius is an air sign, but the Water-carrier, and many Aquarians carry the water of inspiration for others to drink whilst sometimes forgetting that they too need a sip occasionally. Sometimes this quality of eccentric detachment can isolate your child from others in an emotional way, starving them of what they actually need for themselves, so it would be wise to ask them how they really *feel* occasionally. Encourage them to sip and process the water they carry for the benefit of humanity.

Aquarians flourish in groups, clubs, teams and organisations which share a common interest, eventually serving the community with visionary and sometimes lofty ideals. What Aquarius strives for is the Brotherhood of Man, for the spirit of equality burns brightly in their breast. Sometimes they are inept in personal matters of the heart but brilliant at dealing with organisations involving large numbers of people. They will often follow careers that champion the underdogs in our society.

They are both repelled and compulsively attracted to people and situations which display passionate or explosive intensity, and are good arbitrators and diplomats with an inherent ability to see everybody's side of the story. You might experience your little Aquarian trying to be the peacemaker in your home and trying to dispel angry and

Sun

disruptive situations. On a larger scale, the United Nations was set up to become a perfect forum for the Aquarian vision of what mankind could eventually be, yet this whole organisation has had to face many problems because, as a species, we humans are so unable to get along with each other - and even within the UN itself this same divisive energy may be found. Hypocrisy so easily haunts the Aquarian ideal and a parent may need to guide a child through these kinds of issues as they grow up.

Aquarius is a mental or 'concept' sign fixed on the future, so it is sometimes difficult for them to express and release their feelings and emotions to others in a deeply personal way. This can leave them vulnerable to the darker undercurrents of human nature as they feel very uneasy around emotionally loaded situations. Because of this they sometimes avoid or distance themselves from close personal contact. They will tell you when old enough that this is because of their need to treat all their friends with utmost tolerance and fairness. They won't often mention the gut-wrenching fear that emotional involvement gives them, nor their own jealous and possessive streak. Your awareness of this will assist in the parenting process.

Your child's body is sometimes electrically wired to their own light bulb! To make an electrical charge safe it must be earthed, and the realism of the earthy planet and co-ruler Saturn needs to be understood. Until your child is old enough to cope with this by themselves, you can again step in, ground or 'earth' the charge, and balance their highly tuned systems with something very simple and practical, like taking a hot bath, enjoying a cuddle or going for a walk in the countryside. Such activities will help bring them down to earth - which is perhaps the best thing a parent of an Aquarian child can do.

Aquarius

Oh, and then lovingly pack the flask of chicken soup when they next go off into that 'off the planet mode', travelling to those outer frontiers where no man has gone before but where your little astronaut longs to be. (Doctor) Who knows, they may even send you a postcard of the view from space!

MOON IN AQUARIUS

She seems endowed with a strong mind which will protect her from excessive emotion.

George Sand

With the Moon placed here, a parent needs to accommodate a child needing constant reassurance and a feeling of security and safety whilst feeling free to express their autonomy and independence. What a paradox this is and what a responsibility! For whilst your little Aquarian Moon may appear autonomous and overly self-sufficient, or a little alien, no Moon position needs a close and loving parent more than this one. So when your child goes into 'off the planet mode', firing their imaginary rocket ships off into in the sky, don't fret, just play mission control and provide all the life support systems. Be there when they re-enter the earth's atmosphere, and don't get too upset if sometimes they just don't respond to you, then suddenly shock or delight you with their eccentrically funny behaviour. Tune in to your child's special needs and don't feel affronted by the sudden cool detachment of this independent Moon. If you can provide the support and love to encourage your little Aquarian Moon to feel included, they will be only too happy to let you glimpse their colourful visions and experiences.

You will notice that there is a definite maverick quality in this Moon. Try to understand their sense of aloneness and alienation and the feeling of not fitting in and not belonging sometimes. This child will have many moods and many fancies which can result in flights of sheer brilliance for they have many original and magical thoughts which someday will contribute to the comfort and progress of society and mankind. Perhaps they should be given a room of their own where they can practice the principal of detachment away from the emotional demands of other members of the family. Truly, they need to feel part of domestic life, but not enmeshed in it.

Moon

As we move into the Aquarian Age, where the barriers of status, gender, age and class have become increasingly blurred, your Aquarian child will feel more connected and comfortable about what they have come here to do and should be encouraged to express the novelty of

their ideas. Try to accommodate and listen to their zany and unconventional ideas for a progressive future. They will have many friends, from all walks of life, many of them strange and unconventional, and will often flourish in groups, clubs or teams where they can get together with others to share a common interest, anywhere where they can interact with others in a impersonal way.

Aquarians often shy away from the intensity of a personal or passionate relationship. Their interests lie in the quest to discover that perfect friendship with one other, where the boundaries of behaviour are not robustly set in concrete. Relationships that prevent them from expressing their own uniqueness or where they feel emotionally trapped are usually avoided.

This is not to say that your Aquarian Moon does not need intimacy with others. But the manner by which they acquire intimacy may be radically different from anything you've ever imagined. In a birth chart the sign where the Moon is placed indicates what we need to be nourished. A Moon in Aquarius thrives on experiment and change, invention and novelty. A parent needs to provide this in order that the child can feel nourished. If your child appears a little cool and heartless, you might perhaps need to explain that some people obtain their nourishment from being closer and more intimate, but most Aquarians inherently know this anyway. Because of their ability to remain detached from their own personal bias, they make good social commentators, fine negotiators and artists, conveying social statements which serve society, improving the lot of mankind. Beatle John Lennon (Moon in Aquarius) encapsulated this vision of Aquarius in his song *Imagine* - listen to the words and you'll get a good feel of your child's real nature and motivations. Diana, Princess of Wales also had her

Aquarius

Moon in Aquarius, and became 'The People's Princess', doing a job that enabled her to help the outsiders and misfits in society - and helped enormously the victims of AIDS when it was considered distasteful and unfashionable for a person of her position to do so. Her popular title was bestowed on her by another person with his Moon placed in this sign - Tony Blair, whose image of civility and liberalism cuts right across the English class system. They both accept people from all walks of life without evident prejudice.

Be prepared for 'Open House' as your child will probably have lots of friends and your house will sometimes itself seem like the United Nations, a place where they invite their friends from all walks life with every race, colour and creed welcome. You will never be bored with your eccentrically delightful time traveller who strives to make this World a better place for themselves and for mankind. Instead of 'No!', just learn to say, 'Why not?' and life will never be the same again. Enjoy your flight!

ASCENDANT IN AQUARIUS

Here in this circle let us give thanks. Let this circle be a symbol of our purpose where each man is equal to the other, each has a voice and each will strive to fight for truth and honour.

King Arthur in *Merlin*.

If you child has been born with an Aquarian Ascendant they should be given space and scope to contribute something of their revolutionary, liberating and sometimes eccentric minds and imaginations towards the environment and society in which they find themselves. Encourage your child's original and inventive outlook on life and try not to be affronted by their sometimes detached and impersonal manner. It is important that they do not feel cramped or limited and are given a free and unbiased arena in which to express their sometimes maverick personality and where their electric and magnetic presence may be felt. Conversely, it is important to convey to your child that effort should be sustained in attaining discipline and self control, if their unique contribution to their own and other's lives is to be realised. In this imperfect world they'll need steely determination

Ascendant

and much stamina. The traditional ruling planet of this sign, prior to the discovery of Uranus, was realistic and resolute Saturn. Uranus' perverse and self-opinionated style will need tempering down by Saturn's respect of limitations and boundaries if an Aquarian is to succeed on planet Earth.

This Ascendant expresses the need of elevating the love consciousness in mankind to a higher goal than just personal satisfaction. This may be seen in the works of Germaine Greer (Sun and Ascendant in Aquarius) who has strived to elevate the lot of womanhood with her outspoken eccentricity and her radical thinking. Intimate relationships can prove restrictive for such a collectively orientated Ascendant sign, and yet all Aquarians - Sun, Moon or strong planetary placements in the sign - yearn for a society that embodies their vision of a perfect and harmonious planet - which, paradoxically is a collective intimacy, a clue to the following sign, Pisces. The solution to this paradox is not for lesser mortals like parents to solve, but a clue to its solution may be found by studying the shadow side of Aquarius' opposite sign, Leo. Leo rules the heart, and Aquarius needs to find their heart and respond to its needs without letting these overwhelm them.

Aquarius

If your child can balance the needs of the personal ego against those of promoting the common good, then all will be well and you will indeed be the proud parent of a true servant of the people.

FAMOUS AQUARIANS

Sun in Aquarius

Buzz Aldrin, Robert Burns, John Barrymore, Lord Byron, Alice Cooper, Lewis Caroll, Phil Collins, Charles Dickens, Neil Diamond, Placido Domingo, Christian Dior, Thomas Edison, Guy Fawkes, Germaine Greer, Clark Gable, Barry Humphries, John Hurt, James Joyce, Eartha Kitt, Charles A Lindbergh, Abraham Lincoln, Desmond Morris, Edouard Manet, Wolfgang Amadeus Mozart, Jack Nicklaus, Yoko Ono, Boris Pasternak, Mary Quant, John Ruskin, Vanessa Redgrave, Ruth Rendell, Clare Short, Virginia Wolf, Franco Zeffrelli.

Moon in Aquarius

Tony Blair, Bert Bacharach, Joan Crawford, Princess Diana, J.F. Kennedy Jr. Vivien Leigh, George Lucas, Nikolai Lenin, Sophie Loren, John Lennon, Marilyn Monroe, Desmond Morris, David Putnum, Cat Stevens, Richard Wagner, Orson Wells, William Butler Yeats.

Ascendant in Aquarius

Burt Bacharach, Bjorn Borg, Carl G Jung, Marie Curie, Kirk Douglas, William Defoe, F.Scott Fitzgerald, Whoopi Goldberg, Stewart Granger, Germaine Greer, Larry Hagman, Janis Joplin, Spike Milligan, Karl Marx, Nina Simone, Tammy Wynette, William Butler Yeats.

PISCES

Pisces symbolises the two Fishes swimming in opposite directions, one swimming downstream representing the personality, and the other swimming upstream representing the soul and is the 3rd Water Sign.

KEYWORDS: *Romantic, impressionable, dreamers, artistic, compassionate, unfathomable.*

I am a feather for each wind that blows.
Shakespeare, *The Winter's Tale*

Pisces

SUN IN PISCES
(Birthday between February 22nd and March 20th)

Deep in the heart of your little Pisces child lies a romantic, a spinner of dreams and fairy stories. Not all Pisceans reveal this side of their nature, but if you care to delve deep enough, you will find that they have very impressionable and imaginative temperaments. Many Pisceans hide this sensitivity from what they feel is a hard, cruel world in which, unfortunately, they feel engulfed. This is the last of the water signs and Pisceans pick up moods and atmospheres in the environment like we lesser mortals pick up sand off the beach. Most of us are completely and blissfully unaware of such atmospheres, yet because your little angel has this ability, they may often have a shaky sense of their own unique identity. You have an acutely receptive and sympathetic soul on your hands, a little hot house flower who needs sensitive and careful handling. But once you can recognise your child's need to be contained with safety and empathy, fully understanding their deeply compassionate nature, you're half-way to success already. Learn to listen to their dreams, impressions and wonderfully prophetic visions.

Like the chameleon, who takes on all the colours and shapes of the atmosphere around them, Pisceans can be all things to all people, which can be very confusing to everyone, including themselves. But because of this gift they make very fine actors who can get into any character and convey their very essence and soul. It is as well to encourage your little fish to develop a firm sense of *self* in which they can firmly root themselves, so that when they are feeling isolated or misunderstood, or when the strong winds of life blow around them, they are not knocked off centre. Pisceans, like ships at sea, need to know their bearings or they become very vulnerable and disorientated, and may find themselves in dangerous waters.

Like a psychic sponge, they soak up the emotional atmosphere and often feel invaded by those around them. This is why it is important that they are given a quiet place within their environment where no one can stamp on their dreams or pollute the psychic space surrounding them. With such a sensitive antenna to the environment, Pisces children need to periodically recharge their batteries by spending time on their own in a peaceful place. Plenty of sleep and plenty of relaxing baths helps this process. Not that they are weak; for given the right encouragement Pisceans are quite capable of turning their dreams into reality. Like Neptune, their ruler, your little Piscean's temperament will shift and change and be as unfathomable as the ocean. Try and be patient when they slip into one of their silent dreams, they've gone fishing for a while, perhaps to catch that big dream or vision which is buried deep in their unconscious, but which one day they can realise - propelling them to the top of their chosen profession or trade.

Fantasy and dreams are very important to their often inspired poetic minds. It may be thought of as escapist for anyone to daydream or wool-gather in such a way, yet a wise parent will encourage such activity and attempt to guide a child into some kind of focused end-product. In so doing you will encourage your little 'fish' to be like the great salmon, who determinedly swims upstream to release the offspring of their 'creations'. Effort counts, whether it be in finishing a poem, painting or producing a wonderful garden. Vita Sackville West - Sun in Pisces - created her famous 'secret' garden at Sissinghurst through years of effort grounding the dreams and vision she clearly possessed.

It is no surprise that some of our most famous actors, artists and musicians have the sign of Pisces strongly placed in their horoscope and many are drawn to the illusionary world of film, television, photography and dance, anything that enables them to express their fertile imagination, and which helps them escape from the mundane realities of life. Michaelangelo, one of the world's most famous artists, was a Piscean and he struggled with the practical side of life, being dependant on the Pope, his patron, to help him concretise his inspired gifts. Pisces is a mutable sign and it is wise for a parent of a Piscean child to show the balance between the more mundane and practical things of life, and the exploration they must undertake into the more artistic and mystical side of their natures. Because of this need for containment, Pisceans are often attracted to the realistic energy given off by the Earth signs - Taurus, Virgo and Capricorn. These pragmatic people can assist them in grounding their inspired creative visions which will help them to be recognised and rewarded for their creative contributions to the world.

Pisces is the sign of the misunderstood genius and you will sometimes hear your little Pisces saying "one day" a lot - "one day I'm going to be a great actor singer or painter...". But their dreams can be lost and fall by the wayside if they don't get down to the day to day routine of *working* towards the realisation of at least some of their highly creative dreams or visions. Their opposite sign, Virgo, can teach them a great deal in this direction.

You will find your child is acutely sensitive to your emotional life and will often pick up on things that even you are not aware of, but they can touch the deepest places of your soul. It's impossible to keep emotional

secrets from a Pisces, but unlike Scorpio, this water sign is less invasive, and normally they won't invade your emotional space nor challenge you about it, unless they have a large dose of one of the more demonstrative signs in their birthchart. They will just give you a 'knowing' look, which says, "Don't worry, I understand". Let your Pisces take care of you or nurse you sometimes. They like to play the saviours and rescuers of the Zodiac, because they love and indeed thrive when they are of service in this way. Because of this many are drawn to the helping and caring professions. Understand that this is a water sign and Pisceans desperately need to be needed. So show them your vulnerability and they will respond with the utmost care, empathy and compassion.

With their sympathetic and helpful natures, it follows that they can be prone to being invaded or exploited by other less sensitive and intrusive people. Because they have an issue with boundaries - where they end and

Moon

where the outside world begins - they can become overwhelmed to the point where they feel the need to totally escape, which can result in over-consumption of food, drugs and drink. Liz Taylor epitomised this trait, joining with Richard Burton in *Who's Afraid of Virginia Wolf?*, depicting the worst aspects of Piscean excess. Perhaps this is why the sign has such a reputation for sometimes feeling victimised by life. Your child may therefore need help if they drop into the role of the martyr or victim, feeling unable to cope with life

If their sense of self is weak, then a Piscean may attempt to live their life through other people's lives, at the expense of developing their own. There may then be issues with discretion and gossip, which are spin-offs from this lack of a firm identity. Teaching a Piscean child to pick themselves up, dust themselves off and get back into the life-game is the wisest thing a parent can do, but it needs sensitivity. It is possible for a Piscean to be both sensitive and tough, artistic and determined, inspired and decisive - but it may take many mistakes and many rolls of elastoplast to get there. Escaping into confusion and hopelessness is no solution to anything.

This being the last sign of the Zodiac, you may find your child carries the whole world within, and may feel acutely the burdens and sorrows of society. This feeling can be relieved by encouraging them to express the comic side of their natures. Pisces is a natural clown and often has a wonderful sense of humour, but there is always a touch of pathos and sadness about them because of their deep connection to the mess we humans sometimes make of life. Pam Ayres and Tommy Cooper are wonderful examples of this side of Pisces. They are able to unconditionally forgive others for their mistakes and wrongdoings, because of their compassion and deep understanding. This is the great gift that your child brings to you, and the world. In that sense they become the true and humble servants of mankind.

MOON IN PISCES

Why do I feel I want to cry for everybody, forever....?

Anon

When you tuck your little Pisces Moon up in bed at night, get ready to enter the land of their dreams and remember to read them a story which appeals to their 'happy ever after' temperament. Stories delight their romantic imaginations and transport them into a fairy world. Many Pisceans enter the world of film, imagery, advertising and photography to pursue these illusory themes which are, at the same time, so human. Stories of magical islands and deep lagoons, replete with mermaids that disappear and reappear are ideal. Pisceans need to discover and connect to this state of enchantment. Legends of the sea particularly nourish those with this Moon position, for the nature of such stories is as important to them as the real world, for this is where they feel most at home. The sea also contains precious treasures, just like your child's nature. Try to help your little fish indulge in their fantasies by entering into their mystical world for a while and sharing it with them. Neptune is the god of the sea, and the ruling planet of Pisces and like the ocean, this planet is mysterious and unfathomable, and is associated with enchantment, illusion, inspiration and all things nebulous.

Never, never crush the dreams of your Piscean Moon child, or their inspired poetic minds, for one day, if given the right encouragement and support, they are going to make their dreams come true, just like it tells them in the fairy stories. Their reflective and fertile imaginations are one of their greatest resources and their natural deep insights into people and their sensitivity to their environment could result in wonderfully creative output in the form of acting, music, poetry, dance and writing. Joni Mitchell, the 'High Priestess of Song', has her Moon in Pisces and she has inspired the public with her mystical and poetical

Moon

songs. Frank Sinatra and Elvis Presley who poetically interpreted their songs also had their Moon position here. Other Pisceans serve humanity through caring and social work. This Moon's disposition is extremely gentle and impressionable and gives a heightened sensitivity. Not that it cannot be very determined, Helen Keller, the blind and deaf author, had her Moon here, as did the ultra-sensitive poet Shelley.

Your Pisces Moon child will be very aware and emphatic to your emotions and to the atmosphere in the home. This is the best place to begin helping your child to develop stronger boundaries in order to learn to better withstand the impact of negative vibrations around them. They are also particularly sensitive to the suffering and neediness that surrounds them and can identity very strongly with the victim and vulnerable in our society. With their compassionate natures,

they are drawn to the areas of life where they can be of service, helping those who are afflicted, downtrodden or misfits. Sometimes it's important for them to withdraw from life, distancing themselves from their impressions of the sometimes painful, aggressive world. They will one day thank you for providing them with their own private place, perhaps a secret hideaway, where they can quietly process their complex feelings and emotions. If your child suddenly disappears, like the fish, don't be affronted or alarmed, they've just 'gone fishing' for a while, and will rejoin you with all their beautiful fishy colours, ready to nurture and enliven your day with their dreams and impressions.

This is a psychic and subjective Moon and your child will be very sensitive to the emotional undercurrents that run through the family, this is why they need to develop strong boundaries, to protect them when they reach emotional overload. This Moon needs to learn to say "No!" occasionally, as it may feel over obliged to help others in their hour of need, an activity which can lead to a depletion of energy and being completely invaded by other's demands. This will upset their very delicate systems which could lead to feelings of resentment. They need to be encouraged to relax, perhaps while listening to their favourite music, so essential to the well-being of this acutely sensitive Moon. Being near the sea and in touch with tidal rhythms, which are caused and synchronous with the Moon's phases, will nourish their heart and show them that the water element is valued. Mahler typifies this watery connection in his 'Resurrection' symphony. It was even composed in a small hut by a lake - an ideal location for the natural flow of his Piscean Moon and Cancerian Sun. The ruling planet of Pisces is the distant Neptune, once more connecting us to the King of the Ocean, the watery depths from which we all emerge and where we will surely return.

ASCENDANT IN PISCES

A wise man adapts himself to circumstances as water shapes itself to the vessel that contains it.

Chinese Proverb

Like the symbol of the fishes swimming in two different directions, the approach of this Ascendant can be dualistic The fish can either swim upstream or downstream and often this is a true dilemma for this sign. So it cannot be over-stressed that your child needs to be encouraged to become responsible for their own actions, to create a solid identity adequate to deal effectively with the mundane realities of life, developing as practical a nature as their impressionable souls will allow without becoming too influenced by others. This will help them ground themselves in their formative years, enabling them to eventually feel secure enough to devote themselves to the service of society in nurturing roles such as caring for the sick and needy, or in some mystical, musical, creative or artistic way.

Ascendant

All too often the Piscean tendency to 'go with the flow' and letting others make their choices for them, render them vulnerable to being exploited and leaving them 'all at sea'. Just as water always tries to flow downhill, Pisceans can sometimes take the path of least resistance, and need a external container to prevent them from being self-destructive and their energies dissipated. Some Pisceans will tell you that life is an illusion, so why bother? Instead, they will argue, why not try to get back into that womb-like state, back to the Garden of Eden and paradise, where it was at least safe and warm? With this in mind, they need to be encouraged to develop self discipline to realise their potential gift of expressing their considerable creativity in whatever walk of life they choose in the World. This kind of argument needs to be firmly countermanded by a parent, else otherwise it will be difficult for growth or a responsible attitude to life to develop in those important formative years. If the negative approach to life is taken it can lead to increasing resentment which may, in extreme cases, eventually force Pisces into manipulative and victimised behaviour (*"No-one understands me"* or *"Poor little me"*), which should be avoided at all costs if this Ascendant is to provide inspiration to others. And providing inspiration either personally or professionally is the best quality of this Ascending sign.

FAMOUS PISCEANS
Sun in Pisces

Prince Andrew, Prince Edward, W.H. Auden, Paddy Ashdown, Ursula Andress, Harry Belafonte, Alexander Graham Bell, Elizabeth Barrett Browning, Michael Caine, Copernicus, Glenn Close, Edgar Cayce, Neville Chamberlain, Chopin, Johnny Cash, Fats Domino, Roger Daltry, Kenny Dalgleish, Albert Einstein, Bobby Fischer, Peter Fonda, Galileo, Kenneth Grahame, Mikhail Gorbachev, Jean Harlow, Rex Harrison, Douglas Hurd, George Harrison, Victor Hugo, Ibsen, Edward Kennedy, Rimsky Korsakov, Longfellow, Jerry Lewis, Liza Minelli, David Mellor, Glen Miller, Rupert Murdoch, Michaelangelo, John Mills, Nijinsky, Rudolf Nureyev, Anais Nin, Baden Powell, David Putnum, Sam Peckinpah, Samuel Pepys, Sydney Poitier, Maurice Ravel, Lynn Redgrave, Michael Redgrave, Renoir, Nina Simone, John Steinbeck,

Pisces

Johann Strauss, Gloria Vanderbilt, Antonio Vilvaldi, Harold Wilson, Nancy Wilson, Vita Sackville West.

Moon in Pisces

Paddy Ashdown, Enrico Caruso, Errol Flynn, Hugh Hefner, Eartha Kitt, Rimsky Korsakov, Michaelangelo, Joni Mitchell, Prince, Elvis Presley, Maurice Ravel, Franz Shubert, Frank Sinatra, Percy Bysshe Shelley, Robin Williams.

Ascendant in Pisces

Alexander Graham Bell, Whitney Houston, Alfred Hitchcock, Anthony Armstrong Jones, R. D. Laing, Bob Monkhouse, Dean Martin, Robert Redford, Ringo Starr, George Washington, Tennessee Williams.

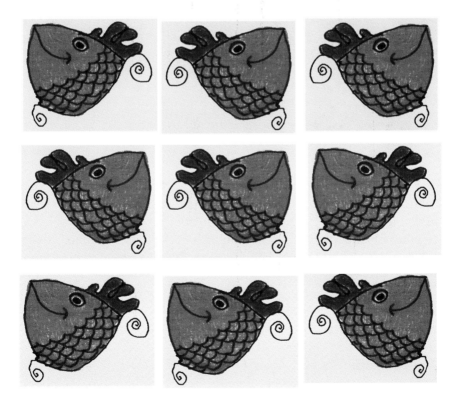

The Zodiac Signs and the Corresponding parts of the body

Aries rules the head

Taurus rules the neck and throat

Gemini rules arms, shoulders and lungs

Cancer rules the stomach

Leo rules the heart and mid-spine

Virgo rules the small intestine

Libra rules the kidneys, renal system and belt line

Scorpio rules the lower bowel, elimination systems & sexual organs

Sagittarius rules the thighs

Capricorn rules the knees

Aquarius rules the lower leg and ankles

Pisces rules the feet.

The statue is of the Egyptian Goddess *Ptai*, who ruled over childbirth and children.

TABLES FOR FINDING THE MOON-SIGN
STAGE ONE: From the Date of Birth, Find the MOON NUMBER

MONTH OF BIRTH

DAY OF BIRTH	JANUARY	Moon Number	FEBRUARY	Moon Number	MARCH	Moon Number	APRIL	Moon Number
	1,2	1	1,2	3	1,2	3	1,2	5
	3,4	2	3,4	4	3,4	4	3,4	6
	5,6	3	5,6	5	5,6	5	5,6	7
	7,8	4	7,8	6	7,8	6	7,8	8
	9,10	5	9,10	7	9,10	7	9,10	9
	11,12	6	11,12,13	8	11,12	8	11,12,13	10
	13,14,15	7	14,15	9	13,14	9	14,15,16	11
	16,17	8	16,17	10	15,16,17	10	17,18	12
	18,19	9	18.19.20	11	18,19	11	19,20,21	1
	20,21	10	21,22,23	12	20,21,22	12	22,23	2
	22,23	11	24,25	1	23,24	1	24,25	3
	24,25,26	12	26,27,28	2	25,26,27	2	26,27,28	4
	27,28,29	1	29	3	28,29	3	29,30	5
	30,31	2			30,31	4		

ROBIN HEATH 1984

MONTH OF BIRTH

DAY OF BIRTH	MAY	Moon Number	JUNE	Moon Number	JULY	Moon Number	AUGUST	Moon Number
	1,2	6	1,2	8	1,2	9	1	10
	3,4	7	3,4	9	3,4	10	2,3	11
	5,6	8	5,6,7	10	5,6	11	4,5,6	12
	7,8	9	8,9	11	7,8,9	12	7,8	1
	9,10	10	10,11,12	12	10,11,12	1	9,10	2
	11,12,13	11	13,14,15	1	13,14	2	11,12,13	3
	14,15,16	12	16,17	2	15,16	3	14,15	4
	17,18	1	18,19	3	17,18	4	16,17	5
	19,20,	2	20,21	4	19,20	5	18,19	6
	21,22	3	22,23	5	21,22,23	6	20,21	7
	23,24,25	4	24,25	6	24,25	7	22,23	8
	26,27	5	26,27	7	26,27	8	24,25	9
	28,29	6	28,29,30	8	28,29	9	26,27,28	10
	30,31	7			30,31	10	29,30,31	11

ROBIN HEATH 1984

MONTH OF BIRTH

DAY OF BIRTH	SEPTEMBER	Moon Number	OCTOBER	Moon Number	NOVEMBER	Moon Number	DECEMBER	Moon Number
	1,2	12	1,2	1	1,2,3	3	1,2	4
	3,4	1	3,4	2	4,5	4	3,4	5
	5,6	2	5,6	3	6,7	5	5,6	6
	7,8,9	3	7,8,9	4	8,9	6	7,8,9	7
	10,11	4	10,11	5	10,11	7	10,11	8
	12,13	5	12,13	6	12,13	8	12,13	9
	14,15	6	14,15	7	14,15	9	14,1516	10
	16,17	7	16,17	8	16,17,18	10	17 18,19	11
	18,19	8	18,19	9	19,20	11	20,21 22	12
	20,21,22	9	20,21	10	21,22,23	12	,23,24	1
	23,24,25	10	22,23,24	11	24,25	1	25,26	2
	26,27	11	25,26	12	26,27,28	2	27 28	3
	28,29	12	27,28,29	1	29,30	3	29,30	4
	30	1	30,31	2			31	5

ROBIN HEATH 1984

Finding the Moon-sign

STAGE TWO - FINDING THE MOON SIGN

In the table below, first look up the YEAR of birth in the left-hand columns. Read across to where the column that shows the MOON NUMBER, as found on the previous page, identifies uniquely the Moon Sign. Because the Moon can and does change sign independently of the calendar day, these tables can only be correct for about 80% of births. It is therefore recommended that a full chart is prepared by a qualified astrologer.

FINDING THE MOON SIGN

MOON NUMBER

BIRTH DATE YEAR			1	2	3	4	5	6	7	8	9	10	11	12
1960	1979	1998	♒	♓	♈	♉	♊	♋	♌	♍	♎	♏	♐	♑
1961	1980	1999	♊	♋	♌	♍	♎	♏	♐	♑	♒	♓	♈	♉
1962	1981	2000	♏	♐	♑	♒	♓	♈	♉	♊	♋	♌	♍	♎
1963	1982	2001	♓	♈	♉	♊	♋	♌	♍	♎	♏	♐	♑	♒
1964	1983	2002	♌	♍	♎	♏	♐	♑	♒	♓	♈	♉	♊	♋
1965	1984	2003	♐	♑	♒	♓	♈	♉	♊	♋	♌	♍	♎	♏
1966	1985	2004	♈	♉	♊	♋	♌	♍	♎	♏	♐	♑	♒	♓
1967	1986	2005	♍	♎	♏	♐	♑	♒	♓	♈	♉	♊	♋	♌
1968	1987	2006	♑	♒	♓	♈	♉	♊	♋	♌	♍	♎	♏	♐
1969	1988	2007	♊	♋	♌	♍	♎	♏	♐	♑	♒	♓	♈	♉
1970	1989	2008	♎	♏	♐	♑	♒	♓	♈	♉	♊	♋	♌	♍
1971	1990	2009	♓	♈	♉	♊	♋	♌	♍	♎	♏	♐	♑	♒
1972	1991	2010	♋	♌	♍	♎	♏	♐	♑	♒	♓	♈	♉	♊
1973	1992	2011	♏	♐	♑	♒	♓	♈	♉	♊	♋	♌	♍	♎
1974	1993	2012	♈	♉	♊	♋	♌	♍	♎	♏	♐	♑	♒	♓
1975	1994	2013	♌	♍	♎	♏	♐	♑	♒	♓	♈	♉	♊	♋
1976	1995	2014	♑	♒	♓	♈	♉	♊	♋	♌	♍	♎	♏	♐
1977	1996	2015	♉	♊	♋	♌	♍	♎	♏	♐	♑	♒	♓	♈
1978	1997	2016	♎	♏	♐	♑	♒	♓	♈	♉	♊	♋	♌	♍

The table above derives from the remarkable fact that, every nineteen years, the Sun and Moon almost exactly repeat their cycles. It is called the Metonic cycle, after the Greek mathematician-astronomer who is alleged to have discovered the cycle over two thousand years ago. After 19 years there have elapsed 235 full moons, and this repeat cycle enables the tables above to furnish the Moon's position for any date.

FINDING THE ASCENDING SIGN

Using this table it is only necessary to simply match the appropriate Sun-sign column with the Birth time. For example, for a Taurean born at 3:34pm, the Ascendant would be Libra, while a Virgo born at 2:28am would have a Leo Ascendant. The Sun-signs Libra to Pisces are found on the following page.

BIRTH TIME	SUN-SIGN					
	ARIES	TAURUS	GEMINI	CANCER	LEO	VIRGO
MIDN - 1 AM	♑	♒	♓	♈♉	♊	♋
1 AM - 2 AM	♑	♓	♈	♉♊	♊♋	♌
2 AM - 3 AM	♒	♓	♉	♊	♋	♌
3 AM - 4 AM	♓	♈	♊	♋	♌	♌
4 AM - 5 AM	♓♈	♉	♊♋	♋	♌	♍
5 AM - 6 AM	♈	♊	♋	♌	♌♍	♍
6 AM - 7 AM	♉	♊♋	♋	♌	♍	♎
7 AM - 8 AM	♉♊	♋	♌	♌	♍	♎
8 AM - 9 AM	♊	♋	♌	♍	♎	♎
9 AM - 10 AM	♊♋	♋	♌	♍	♎	♏
10 AM - 11 AM	♋	♌	♍	♎	♎	♏
11 AM - NOON	♋♌	♌	♍	♎	♏	♐
NOON - 1 PM	♌	♍	♍	♎	♏	♐
1 PM - 2 PM	♌	♍	♎	♏	♏	♐
2 PM - 3 PM	♍	♍	♎	♏	♐	♑
3 PM - 4 PM	♍	♎	♏	♏	♐	♑
4 PM - 5 PM	♍	♎	♏	♐	♑	♒
5 PM - 6 PM	♎	♏	♏♐	♐	♑	♓
6 PM - 7 PM	♎	♏	♐	♑	♒	♈
7 PM - 8 PM	♏	♏	♐	♑	♓	♈♉
8 PM - 9 PM	♏	♐	♑	♒	♈	♉♊
9 PM - 10 PM	♏	♐	♑	♒♓	♈	♊♋
10 PM - 11 PM	♐	♑	♒	♓	♉	♊♋
11 PM - MIDN	♐	♑	♒♓	♈	♉♊	♋

FINDING THE ASCENDING SIGN
(Signs Libra to Pisces)

BIRTH TIME	SUN-SIGN					
	LIBRA	SCORPIO	SAGITR	CAPRICN	AQUARI	PISCES
MIDN - 1 AM	♌	♍	♎	♎	♏	♐
1 AM - 2 AM	♌	♍	♎	♏	♏	♐
2 AM - 3 AM	♍	♎	♎	♏	♐	♑
3 AM - 4 AM	♍	♎	♏	♏	♐	♑
4 AM - 5 AM	♍	♎	♏	♐	♑	♒
5 AM - 6 AM	♎	♏	♏	♐	♑	♒♓
6 AM - 7 AM	♎	♏	♐	♐♑	♒	♓
7 AM - 8 AM	♏	♐	♐	♑	♓	♈
8 AM - 9 AM	♏	♐	♑	♒	♓♈	♉
9 AM - 10 AM	♐	♐	♑	♓	♈	♊
10 AM - 11 AM	♐	♑	♒	♓♈	♉	♊♋
11 AM - NOON	♐	♑	♓	♈♉	♊	♋
NOON - 1 PM	♑	♒	♈	♉	♊♋	♋
1 PM - 2 PM	♑	♓	♈♉	♊	♋	♌
2 PM - 3 PM	♒	♈	♉	♊♋	♋	♌
3 PM - 4 PM	♓	♈	♊	♋	♌	♌
4 PM - 5 PM	♓♈	♉	♊	♋	♌	♍
5 PM - 6 PM	♈♉	♊	♋	♌	♌♍	♍
6 PM - 7 PM	♉	♊	♋	♌	♍	♍
7 PM - 8 PM	♉♊	♋	♌	♌	♍	♎
8 PM - 9 PM	♋	♋	♌	♍	♎	♎
9 PM - 10 PM	♋	♋♌	♌	♍	♎	♏
10 PM - 11 PM	♋	♌	♍	♎	♏	♏
11 PM - MIDN	♌	♌	♍	♎	♏	♏

Note that these ascendant tables can only be accurate in about 80% of births to which they are applied. To be certain of the Ascending Sign you will need to ask a competent astrologer to erect a birth chart for the child.

Some Examples to Try

EXAMPLE INTERPRETATIONS

On page (vii) may be found descriptions of the meanings of Sun, Moon and Ascendant in the chart. Here is an example of how to blend those meanings. Julius, my first grandchild, was born on the 22nd December, 2002, London at 6:12 am. Using the tables given here check that you agree that Julius's Sun is placed in Capricorn, his Moon is placed in Cancer and his Ascending Sign is Sagittarius. (*or Capricorn, see note at bottom of table opposite*). Read the meanings listed in the main body of the book and then compare it with the brief analysis below.

Brief Analysis - *The sensitive, changeable and creative qualities of the Moon in Cancer are deeply attached to the security and stability of the home life. This needs to be balanced with a strong drive to achieve worldly success and status through the professional life, as indicated by the Capricorn Sun. The path taken to achieve a balance of these two energies would need to incorporate the qualities and perspectives of the Sagittarian Ascendant. This will involve engaging a strong appetite for exploring life to the full, through travel, higher education and understanding the wider meaning of life. A realistic channel should be found to balance the energies of this fiery Sagittarian outlook with the earthy qualities of the Capricorn Sun. To assist in this process Julius should be encouraged to finish projects and to become realistic in his goals. This in turn will need to be tempered with his prime need for a secure home life, as indicated by the Cancer Moon.*

It is a valuable exercise to develop this technique of blending the Sun, Moon and Ascendant positions of the famous and historical people, listed below. Such a gift will enable you to understand better what drives the motives and actions of people in the public eye, and this skill is readily transferable into a rewarding exploration of your own birth chart and the charts of your children, friends and family.

Woody Allen - Sun in Sagittarius, Moon in Aquarius, Ascendant in Virgo.

Tony Blair - Sun in Taurus, Moon in Aquarius, Ascendant Gemini.

HRH Prince Charles - Sun in Scorpio, Moon in Taurus, Ascendant in Leo.

Winston Churchill - Sun in Sagittarius, Moon in Leo, Ascendant Virgo.

Diana, Princess of Wales - Sun in Cancer, Moon in Aquarius, Ascendant Sagittarius.

HRH Queen Elizabeth II - Sun in Taurus, Moon in Leo, Ascendant in Capricorn.

Steven Spielberg - Sun in Sagittarius, Moon in Scorpio, Ascendant in Cancer.

Sir Patrick Moore - Sun in Pisces (conjunct Uranus), Moon in Libra, Ascendant in Gemini.

More About
Sun, Moon & Ascendant

THE MOON
How we nourish ourselves
and 'feel at home'

The Moon rules the sign of Cancer

The Moon is a most important planet in Astrology, for it is connected to our basic survival instincts and how we express our immediate needs, feelings and emotions, and is considered a feminine planet and it symbolises how we nurture and protect ourselves.

The Moon connects us to our ancestry and what we inherit from our family, particularly the relationship to our Mother (or carer) and how she nurtured and cared for us during infancy. The placement of the Moon in a horoscope tells us what we need to feel safe and secure in our environment. A child's first concern is survival and to feel that they belong. The Moon indicates how we feel 'at home' in situations, as what we take into our systems, physically, mentally and emotionally is extremely important to our well-being.

The Moon's cycle was very important to ancient civilisations who regulated their culture by the $29^{1/2}$ day cycle of the new, waxing, full and waning moon. Carved bones have been found notched with 29 or 30 notches, dating back 50,000 years. The Moon is still considered the most important planet in some eastern agricultural cultures, and the lunar 'year' of 354 days (12 full moons) still determines the Islamic religious calendar, whereas for astrologers practising in the western World, which holds to a 'solar' based cultural life, the Sun is now truly the centre of the Solar System.

THE SUN
What we are trying
to become

The Sun rules the sign of Leo

The Sun is connected to the will and our sense of personal identity and creative expression - what we are here to achieve in this lifetime, what we are trying *to become*. The Sun is now the centre of our solar system and is the source of all warmth, light and, ultimately, life itself. The Sun in the horoscope will indicate how, as individuals, we experience our personal Father and our relationship to him and eventually to our relationship with our unique creative spirit. Wherever the Sun is in the horoscope is where we want to shine brightly. The Sun will give us some idea of what our personal journey through life will be like, the task being to develop the qualities and potential indicated by the energy of the Sun, and where it is placed at birth. When we have found the path to the Sun, we are truly expressing our creative life force from the heart.

THE ASCENDANT
The path we follow in Life

The Ascendant in the horoscope is the approach we need to take on this journey through life. The energy and qualities of the Ascendant need to be developed and integrated into the life together with the qualities of the other planets, but particularly the Sun and the Moon. To summarise, the qualities as represented by the Sun need to be developed in our professional lives - the qualities of the Moon need to be developed in our personal lives, whilst the Ascendant shows the path taken to blend the solar and lunar energies, thus enabling us to live as whole individuals and thereby facilitate the very best use of our potential. It is very important that a parent tries to understand the synthesis of this combination in relationship to their developing child. The Ascendant is also like a lens through which we view the world and the environment into which we have arrived.

Connected with the Ascendant is the Midheaven, another important point on the horoscope, one which determines how other people experience us and how we may best project ourselves into the world - through career and our 'public face'.

The Elements

About the Elements and Planets

This book is an elementary introduction to what is a vast and time honoured subject. Here, we have introduced you to the Sun, Moon and Ascendant blend within a horoscope, but as you will discover from the two examples given later in this book (*page 136 onwards*), there are many other 'actors on the stage' within the sphere of our life's journey, these being indicated by all the planets in the birth chart, and their relationship to one another.

The elements of Fire, Earth, Air and Water have long been used in the esoteric traditions and are also very useful in helping us to understand the subtle and powerful energies that surround us in our daily lives. The planets were once thought of as Gods by ancient civilisations, but today modern astrologers understand them as representing inner drives and motivations within the individual, which connect us to our own unique energy and to the ongoing cycles of life.

A Birth chart is a whole representation of a moment of time at a given location or place. While the essential character is shown by the positions of the Sun, Moon and Ascendant, where they are placed on the chart (the astrological 'house') is also important, though beyond the scope of this book. However, in order to entice the reader to further explore this remarkable subject, there follows a general description of the balancing elements and all the planets which an astrologer has to synthesise in a horoscope when preparing a consultation. The understanding of the energy of the planets and the elements can symbolically connect a person to their inner and outer 'universe' in a very rich, insightful way.

Each of the planets must be taken into account if a full picture is to emerge of the character and potentials of an individual with particular placements on their natal chart. For example, on the previous page is given the Sun, Moon and Ascendant positions for astronomer and TV personality Sir Patrick Moore (*see page 125*). An astrologer, seeing that his Sun is conjunct (placed next to) Uranus, sees a clear signature of the remarkable life purpose and career of this popular, eccentric and well loved icon of astronomy.

THE ELEMENTS

- FIRE -

THE FIRE SIGNS ARE ARIES, LEO AND SAGITTARIUS

The element of fire is creative, hot tempered, dramatic and can exhibit great warmth. Fire sign people have natural confidence and optimism, and they express things from the heart. These are the 'children' of the Zodiac and their approach to life is often that of an innocent child, ready for excitement and surprise. The fire type is intuitive and their hunches can turn into a great vision if it can be actualised in the here and now, rationalised and concretised. The fire type is often considered self centred and insensitive, but this is because to find our own centres and be in tune with ourselves, we sometimes need to be *self-ish*. A friend of mine who has a great deal of fire in her chart has this wonderful expression "I'm fired up and running", ready for action. Anything is possible for the fiery types.

Aries gives birth to the vision and pioneers a process, Leo consolidates the vision and manages it, whilst Sagittarius promotes the process enabling it to reach it's full potential.

- EARTH -

THE EARTH SIGNS ARE TAURUS, VIRGO AND CAPRICORN

Earthy types are practical, productive, supportive and patient and are very much in touch with their senses. They look for reality in life and value things that endure and stand the test of time. If you are an earthy person, or someone trying to develop and work with these qualities, try standing barefoot in the garden to experience how good it feels to have contact with the solid earth under your feet. How good it feels to see the fruits of your labours, particularly if you have planted vegetables which provide food, or a tree which finally yields fruit, seemingly without effort. Of course, that earlier care, planning and preparation has enabled the whole process to follow through.

The Elements

Earthy people have great discipline and persistence in pursuing their goals. Their earthy natures like to develop skills to use in the World which will enable them to get what they want from life and more important, to feel secure and safe within their environment to which they are extremely sensitive.

Taurus develops the potential of our raw material (talents and resources), Virgo sorts and synthesises the material, eventually developing and perfecting the skills needed and learning how to use the tools of the trade in question, whilst Capricorn manages that material and performs in the World to refine resources and talents.

- AIR -

THE AIR SIGNS ARE GEMINI, LIBRA AND AQUARIUS

With the element of Air we meet the detached, cultured idealistic people whose progressive ideas attempt to improve the World. These questioning people value the clarity of the word and the mind. They always look for a perfect, balanced outlook on life. There is a great emphasis on justice and humanity and the non-personal, as the Air signs try to rise above our basic, more instinctual nature. This can create problems for the air person, particularly where affairs of the heart are concerned, for if we look at the World from the sky, then we ought to naturally gain a much broader perspective of life. The airy person will always look for peace and harmony and the civilised viewpoint. Sometimes this may seem a little cool, but the element of Air finds it frightening to be confronted by too much irrationality and dark emotions. Airy people sometimes give the impression of being eternally young with their bright, fresh outlook on life and when we feel bogged down or depressed with life, it would be wise to develop their qualities of clear sightedness and detachment, so that we can share in breathing in that wonderful fresh air.

Gemini is concerned with communication and transfer of information and ideas, and the early development and education of the mind. Libra shares the ideas through negotiating in business partnerships and personal relationships, whilst Aquarius takes collective potential and vision of new ideas into the group and society as a whole.

– WATER –

THE WATER SIGNS ARE CANCER, SCORPIO AND PISCES

The element of Water leads us to the vulnerable, instinctual, emotional, imaginative and sensitive side of life. Water looks to the mysteries and hidden depths of life. If you look at the symbols for the water signs, they are all very ancient 'primitive' creatures, the crab, the serpent and the fish. They are in touch with and have empathy for the complexity of human nature and the underlying motives behind people's actions. Because they are intuitive and feeling rather than logical, it is often hard for them to articulate their findings about a situation. Having great empathy and understanding makes them excellent healers, counsellors and artists.

One of the main problems water types have is that they find it difficult to create boundaries, for they absorb people's pain and feel responsible for their problems. This is why it is so important for them to have a private reflective place of their own where their own emotional needs are met and where they can heal themselves. Without the element of water there would be no close, personal connections between people, thus creating an isolated World. Water types need to be needed, otherwise they feel resentful and undernourished. Music is a great relaxant for the water types because their emotions and moods can then be expressed without words.

Cancer learns to stabilise deep personal feelings, often rooted in our past and upbringing, through nurturing and creative action. Scorpio processes those feelings and needs through relationships bringing intense and penetrating interchange, whilst Pisces, being sensitive to the needs and emotions of the whole of Society, works within this, responding to the collective needs of our society.

About the Planets

 # MERCURY

- rules the signs of Gemini (Air) and Virgo (Earth)

Mercury connects us to the magic of words, language and communication helping us link thinking, words, actions and results. It indicates our attitude to early education and the way we learn and absorb information. Our early experiences with brothers and sisters are also under Mercurys rulership and will connect us to the way we experience our local, immediate environment.

Young or old, people with a strong Mercury in their birth chart have a highly curious nature and hunger for knowledge which keeps them eternally young and interested in everyone and everything well into maturity. One 73 year old student of mine said that, "If you learn something each day it means one less wrinkle".

 # VENUS

- rules Taurus (Earth) and Libra (Air)

The desire to co-operate and relate to others in a harmonious way all come under the domain of Venus, as does the balanced understanding of how to use money and resources through good stewardship. Here the ability and drive to create harmony and balance, and relate to others will be very powerful if Venus is strongly placed in the horoscope. Relationships, or the art of relating can be one of our toughest tests in life and usually Venus people are very skilled negotiators and diplomats. They instinctively know how to handle and balance energy in their personal and professional relationships.

A sense of self-worth (*Taurus*) is at the core of any good relationship (*Libra*), enabling each partner to respond to what they each value in a relaxed way, therefore strengthening any relationship, without undermining it, as is often the case when we are not expressing what we value and need most from each other.

MARS

- rules Aries and is the traditional ruler of Scorpio

With the planet Mars we connect to and find our ability and drive to assert ourselves, this enabling us to get what we want from life - what one of my teachers called "taking on the opponent without strain". It indicates how we might be able to distinguish the self from others. The placement of Mars in a horscope will indicate how we find the courage and dynamic energy to start a project and see it through to completion. People with Mars highlighted in their charts are active, forceful and competitive, and may be aggressive. They know what they want and waste no time in letting you know where they stand in a situation. This can lead to relationships of greater honesty, integrity and inner peace. Martian energy renews the life force and forces the sap to rise in plants in the Spring, giving rise to vitality and sexual energy in animals and humans. Both Venus and Mars are about developing a strong set of individual values which equip us to survive despite parental and collective pressure to conform and acquiesce our own needs for those of others or society.

JUPITER

- rules Sagittarius and is the traditional ruler of Pisces

Jupiter urges us to expand and grow through exploration. Wherever Jupiter is placed in the horoscope is where we usually experience good luck and optimism. This gives us the ability to grow throughout our lives which brings wisdom learned through life's varied and rich experiences. In fact the French word *sagesse* means wisdom or 'the wise one'. Jupitarian people are always travelling, either inner or outer - for their ultimate aim in life is to find a belief system so that they can connect to life on a deeper level, enabling them to interact meaningfully and morally with society and their fellow men.

SATURN

- rules Capricorn and is the co-ruler of Aquarius

As Jupiter expands and gives us the opportunity to grow, then Saturn teaches us to consolidate and ground our experiences, reaping the rewards through the passage of time and patient, controlled discipline. It also tells us how we deal with the establishment, authority figures, parents, the boss and the law.

The Planets

With Saturn we learn responsibility, commitment, maturity and self-discipline - for the most solid and valuable lessons learned in life are those based on our most painful and difficult lessons and experiences. Saturn teaches us to become realistic. The placement and sign in which Saturn is placed will tell us where we experience a sense of inferiority and where we are driven, often through frustrating experiences to finally develop a set of values based on reality, accepting our own limitations. This ultimately can confer upon us grace and wisdom.

All the great Mayan Temples in Mexico are built with their steps knee high. Saturn rules the knees, reminding us that the higher we climb, the more humility and grace we need to carry out our duties and responsibilities. If we can understand the irony of this testing energy, then we are truly blessed.

The final three large planets in the solar system have all been discovered in the last two hundred and twenty years, long after astrology was first being used and applied under Babylonian and Egyptian skies. Uranus was discovered in 1781, Neptune in 1846, and Pluto in 1930. They are not visible to the naked eye, and modern astrology considers them to provide a non-personal or collective influence within a horoscope.

 # URANUS

- rules Aquarius together with the planet Saturn

After the stern and sobering lessons of Saturn, we become free to meet the progressive and revolutionary planet of Uranus, where we seek a sense of individuality and originality in our lives. Uranus reaches beyond the realistic limitations of Saturn, inducing us to explore new horizons and possibilities. People with a strong Uranus have a vision of how society should be if we could all strive to be equal, uniting humans across cultures, nationalities and races, impelling them to go beyond and explore new horizons opening up new frontiers of experience. As we enter the Age of Aquarius, we will all be confronted with this ethic in the years to come, and will need to use our sense of tolerance and detachment. This will enable humanity to serve the health and welfare of the planet for the greater common good, creating a true 'Brotherhood of Man'.

Many politicians and famous humanitarians, both past and present, have this planet or sign strongly placed in their horoscopes. Princess Diana, Marie Curie, Carl Jung, Tony Blair and John Lennon (Moon in Aquarius) and John Major (Mars in Aquarius, ruler of his Sun in Aries) to name but a few.

NEPTUNE
- rules the sign of Pisces

The planet Neptune has strong associations with the sea and Neptunian people usually have a deep connection and longing to return to a place where there is no conflict, a place where they can transcend and escape from the banalities of ordinary life and be at one with the Universe. This sense of oneness (wholeness) is usually found through some form of artistic expression - acting, music, dance, mime, poetry and painting.

Here we meet the dreamer of dreams, the mystic, the psychic and healer. Neptunian compassion is boundless, like the ocean. Because of the gentleness and sensitivity associated with this energy, it is very important for the Neptunian type of nature to develop strong boundaries and a strong sense of realism, thereby avoiding constant invasion from others and the outside world.

PLUTO
- rules the sign of Scorpio

In Pluto we meet the urge towards transformation through elimination. In the Tarot, the card of death, when read symbolically, is seen as a card of liberation where we let go of the past, clearing the way for a new beginning. We meet such experiences many times throughout our lives. With the planet Mars, we find our personal power, but people with Pluto strongly emphasised in their birth chart must learn how to share power with others. If this energy is working well, Pluto people usually know how to empower others in their daily lives engendering enriching experiences of positive confrontation, regeneration and new growth. This energy enables them to dig down deep inside their soul for the truth, deepening contact with others. There can be no pretence, ego-aggrandisement or self delusion with Pluto.

Example Charts

EXAMPLE CHART ONE - GIRL

(Full birth data has been withdrawn for confidentiality)

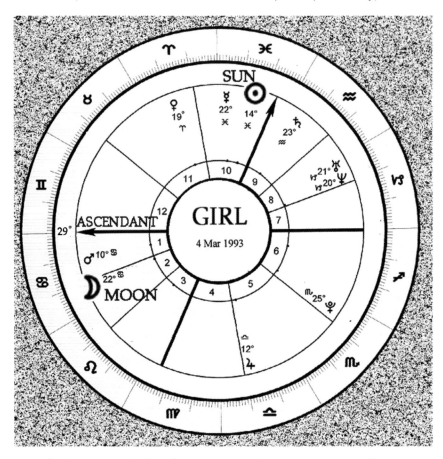

Example Chart One - Blending the meanings of the Sun, Moon & Ascending Signs is a skill gained only after some considerable effort. Using the descriptions in the book, try interpreting yourself from the positions given in the above chart. Then read Helena's interpretation below.

FROM THE CHART, CONFIRM THAT THE MOON IS IN CANCER, THE SUN IS IN PISCES AND THE ASCENDANT IS IN THE SIGN OF GEMINI

When looking at the Birth Charts of children, I always like first to look at the position of the Moon in the horoscope. This immediately enables me to identify the child's immediate needs, and how its parents can supportively tune in to those needs, thereby forming a strong bond with their child at this crucial early stage of development.

As stressed so many times in this book, those early impressionable years are so fundamental to the child's ability to form a trusting relationship to it's parents or carers and eventually to the World around them.

So let us first take a look at the Cancer Moon and see how this child needs to be 'fed' on every level, and what she needs from her mother or primary carer. The Moon in the watery sign of Cancer is an extremely sensitive placement for the Moon and is in its 'dignity', that is, placed in its own sign. With her Sun in the sign of Pisces, another water sign, she is what is called a *double* Water Sign. This endows her with acute emotional and aesthetic sensitivity, particularly to her early surroundings and environment.

This Moon child *needs* lots of emotional assurance from her Mother and placed in the second house of the horoscope, her sense of safety and security will depend on how the Mother copes with her child's need for regular feeding, both physically and emotionally. Touch is most important here and I would strongly recommend that her Mother gives lots and lots of cuddles and demonstrative affection - spending as much time with her child as her daily schedule will allow.

With the Moon in Cancer and placed in the second house, there could be issues around mothering that go right back into the family background - either too much mothering or too little. Either way the figure of 'Mother' is enormous, and I would recommend that both parents are aware of this and perhaps consider their own backgrounds in their relationship to their child. This child will be deeply aware of the emotional undercurrents that pass between her parents and her ancestors which strongly connect her to what has or has not been emotionally processed by them. Bearing this in mind, this child needs to be given a strong sense of caring for and nurturing her own body, which will bring a sense of physical and emotional security throughout her life. This Moon is traditionally very family orientated and loves to feel part of their 'tribe', but this will eventually need to be balanced with her parents encouraging her to express what she deeply values and what she needs *as an individual* in her own right, being a member of a powerful family unit, but not feeling devoured or smothered by them.

Having looked at the needs of the Moon in the Birth Chart, let us now proceed to what the position of the Sun in Pisces has to say. The Sun's position in the horoscope tells us where we want to 'shine' and is linked to the hero's or heroine's journey in Myth. In this Chart, the Sun is placed in the 10th House of the horoscope indicating that on some level she will feel strongly that she wants to seek professional status/recognition in the world.

Example Charts

When a child's Sun is placed in the prestigious 10th house of the horoscope, there is often a history of successful parents, the talents of which the child naturally inherits. There is a drive to achieve which is fuelled by ambitious parents who want their offspring to bring fame and honour to the family, particularly to the dominant parental figure, as this placement is often called the house of 'the Stage Mother/Father'. I would recommend with this placement that the child be encouraged to achieve in the outer world, but also recommend that the parents are sensitive to their child's own unique identity, and not unconditionally expect their child to mirror them. It is important that the child is directed to perform before the world in some capacity, but with an eye on doing it for HERSELF and not just to win her parent's love and admiration, as is often the case with this Sun placement. This is often a difficult balance to strike, but either way, the Sun placed in the artistic, compassionate and magical sign of Pisces endows this child with the potential to be a inspirational person, lifting people's spirits as she journeys through her life.

This child will have a very strong physical presence with the fiery, hot planet Mars placed in the first house of her horoscope. The first house denotes the kind of immediate impact we make on others and with Mars here, she will be difficult to ignore. She should be encouraged to take up some kind of physical regime where she can compete and win (Mars likes to win), thereby releasing some of her powerful energy in a highly structured and disciplined way. Left unchannelled it could get her into some troublesome, argumentative situations with others.

Mars needs a good fight, but Mars should always be encouraged to fight cleanly, particularly when placed in Cancer - for Cancer takes things so personally. It is important too with this placement, that she be encouraged to develop grace and a certain amount of humility in her dealings with others, particularly influential and professionally connected figures. One of the tests of the Sun placed in the 10th House is that if she seeks fame and power throughout her life in whatever capacity, she should use that energy with discretion and integrity, empowering herself and others as she climbs to the top of her own personal mountain.

Lastly, let us look at her Gemini Ascendant which needs to be balanced with her Moon and Sun energies. With a Gemini Ascendant she should be encouraged to express herself to others in a clear and concise way, as distinguishing truth from fantasy is important here. Particularly as Mercury, her Ruler is in retrograde motion at the time of her birth. Mercury placed in the same sign as her Sun is blessed with a wonderfully creative and fertile imagination which needs to be grounded if some of those ideas are to be realised. Her Sun and Moon placed in the non-verbal signs of Cancer and

Pisces, where mood and nuances are used to communicate, sometimes makes it difficult to access feelings which are buried deep within the individual. Often the child feels that their mind is not their own, and can be overpowered by others around them, perhaps feeling that they are the property of their family. Both Cancer and Pisces absorb the atmosphere around them in their need to be included/needed, often attempting to be all things to all people, rather than stand up for what they most need and want.

This airy, objective Ascendant is a good counterpart to her watery, subjective Sun and Moon, enabling her to rise above her sometimes teeming emotions and get some kind of objectivity in any given situation. Learning to listen and to be listened to, particularly by both her parents and the rest of the Family will be important here. Often the child with Mercury retrograde does not feel that they are being heard by the people around them, particularly in their early environment, which can lead to withdrawal and isolation for the child.

Mercury in Pisces has a very fertile and creative imagination and with a Gemini Ascendant, the ability to communicate this by giving the child a grounded early education, with particular emphasis on the arts, would be very beneficial to this child. Issues around siblings need to be understood and talked about within the family, thus avoiding the escalation of natural sibling rivalry which could lead to emotional suffering for this child if not checked. With Mars in Cancer in the first house, she should learn to forcefully express how she feels without getting into potentially messy situations which could undermine her friendships, which will be very important to her as she develops.

The ruler of her Ascendant is in the 10th House of the horoscope (the parental house) which indicates that perhaps her mother had this same problem with her own mother - so this is a very important issue for the whole family to hold up to the light, expose and vanquish. Her ability to communicate and really be HEARD needs to be developed and redeemed. She will then have the potential and the ability to inspire and uplift others through some form of artistic and deeply connected creative expression.

Example Charts

EXAMPLE CHART TWO - BOY
(Full birth data has been withdrawn for confidentiality)

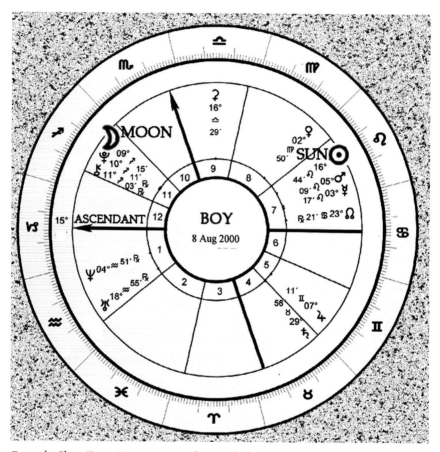

Example Chart Two - Here is a second example for you to try. Using the descriptions in the book, try to blend the three descriptions in the text before reading the descriptive interpretation given here.

CONFIRM FOR YOURSELF THAT THE MOON IS IN SAGITTARIUS, THE SUN IS IN LEO AND THE ASCENDANT IS IN CAPRICORN.

To quote the parents on the arrival of their child who said his arrival "was just a joy" - and with the Sun placed in the charismatic and royal sign of Leo, you would expect that kind of comment from proud parents.

Firstly, let us look at the qualities of his Moon in Sagittarius and how he will need to be nurtured during his early crucial developmental years. This Moon placement endows him with a very friendly, optimistic, inspirational and enthusiastic nature and from an early age will experience many people from all walks of life and nationalities coming and going into his young life. The Moon is placed in the very social 11th House of the horoscope and which indicates that his Mother has a very busy social calendar mixing with many powerful and influential friends and business associates. Although he is already 'programmed' to the demands that others make on his Mother's time, it is important that she give his fiery Moon and Leo Sun all the attention it needs, and will in fact demand.

As he gets older, this is where he will naturally feel 'at home' for there is a tremendous potential to be inspired by one's friends and eventually, to inspire them in making their hopes and dreams for the future come true in some kind of promotional, creative capacity.

As a double fire sign he also has the capacity to be an entrepreneur perhaps in Show Business, as both his parents are involved in this business. Both his Leo and Sagittarius energy needs to be 'on stage' and are known as the actors or showmen of the Zodiac. This child will have a natural talent to inspire others and eventually to be a charismatic leader. The Moon in Sagittarius likes to do everything in a BIG way and feels very frustrated with anything that is considered mediocre. So getting him to keep active through something physically and mentally challenging and which appeals to his romantic nature, would be a good educational investment.

This is a very 'hungry' Moon, with a massive appetite for all the bounteous experiences that life can offer. So it would be a wise parent who can keep an eye on these appetites, encouraging the use of control and discipline in all endeavours. The child will certainly need an expansive, eclectic and universal education which will guide his questing spirit and enable him to understand and learn about those cultures and countries to which one day he will surely travel.

Now let us take a look at the Sun in Leo. Leo is the sign of Kings and Queens and wanting to feel really special and unique in every way. This child also has the planets Mercury and Mars placed in his Sun's sign and these are opposite the imaginative and mystical planet Neptune. This combination is associated with imaginative writing and story telling which should enable him to express himself in a very dramatic and creative way.

The Sun is placed in the Western section of the horoscope in the 7th House. This means that he was born around sunset, traditionally referred to as the 'happy hour', a time when people normally get together to socialise and have a good time together. The 7th House is also associated with the quality of balance and what we share with others. It also indicates that he will inherit great charm and grace and good looks from his parents who are indeed very beautiful people. The Sun placed here also indicates that he has the potential to be a good diplomat and negotiator in all forms of personal or professional relationships. The test of the Sun placed in the 7th House is one of compromise - finding the middle ground in any situation without losing a sense of self. Success here will depend on his ability to use his Leo energy genuinely from the heart, and not from the need to control others.

The fire signs are not known for their ability to compromise, especially when it means sharing the stage with others, but with the Sun placed here, there will be a powerful challenge to truly share his energy in a temperate and empowering way. This will enable him to become a formidable, strong and spirited negotiator in anything he chooses to do throughout his life. However, if the overbearing, bombastic side of Leo appears in his personal or professional dealings with others, then this will be one of his toughest tests in his dealings with others.

Lastly, we look at the Ascendant. With the powerful and sober sign of Capricorn on the Ascendant balancing the exuberant and self-willed energy of his Sagittarius Moon and Leo Sun, his path through life will be that of learning discipline and control. This Ascendant endows him with the ability to approach life's challenges in a practical and persistent way. The drive for success and recognition is very strong here, but the test here is to achieve this with grace and humility as he matures. Here he has the ability to command respect and validation from his peers if he cultivates fairness and integrity which is one of the gifts bestowed by this Ascendant. The sign of Capricorn has strong connections with father and the paternal line, and what this represents to the child. Giving *form* to his creations will be important too. He will be very sensitive to his father's professional life and may perhaps feel isolated sometimes because of his father's absence in the home in his formative years of which one of the causes might be his father's heavy work schedule.

Either way, father and son are a very strong theme here and it will be interesting to see how this develops throughout the child's life. This child has the ability to inspire, bring joy and creative support to those he meets during his life. This, of course, will depend on his parent's ability to bring out the best potentials in him by encouraging him to develop his leadership skills to their fullest capacity.

Taking matters further....

I hope that this is not the end, rather the beginning of your own study of the rich insights which astrology offers. It takes many years study and experience to become competent at reading a birthchart. Whilst this book will explain the key motivations and drives within the horoscope, enabling a parent to better understand their child, the reader who wishes to take the subject further may wish to contact one of the addresses listed below to obtain details of astrology teaching courses, further information or the name of a qualified astrologer in your area.

The Astrological Association
Lee Valley Technopark,
Tottenham Hale,
LONDON
N17 9LN

Midheaven Bookshop
396, Caledonian Road
LONDON
N1 1DN

email: office@astrological.association.co.uk
email: midheaven@compuserve.com

or contact the Hermes Centre
email: hhermespan@aol.com

The Astrologer's Prayer

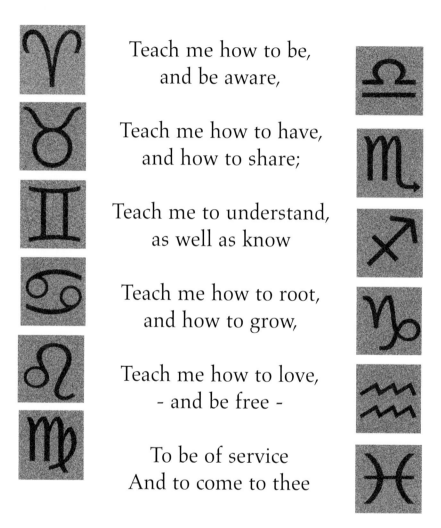

Teach me how to be,
and be aware,

Teach me how to have,
and how to share;

Teach me to understand,
as well as know

Teach me how to root,
and how to grow,

Teach me how to love,
- and be free -

To be of service
And to come to thee

Rev. Pamela Ann Frances Crane
(by kind permission)

FOR YOUR NOTES

NAME	SUN	MOON	ASCENDANT

Published by Bluestone Press, St Dogmaels, Cardigan, Wales
Printed by Gomer Press, Llandysul, Ceredigion, Wales.